YOUR LIFE iS
YOUR PRAYER

Turner Publishing Company
Nashville, Tennessee
www.turnerpublishing.com

Your Life Is Your Prayer: Wake Up to the Spiritual Power in Everything
You Do

Cover Design: Jermaine Lau

Layout & Design: Morgane Leoni

Content on p.143, Worth Circle Diagram © 2009 Suzanne Lorenz and
Sam Beasley

Library of Congress Cataloging-in-Publication number: 2019935685 ISBN:
(print) 978-1-63353-970-9, (ebook) 978-1-63353-971-6

BISAC category code OCC011020 BODY, MIND & SPIRIT / Healing / Prayer
& Spiritual

Printed in the United States of America

YOUR LIFE IS
YOUR PRAYER

WAKE UP TO THE SPIRITUAL
POWER IN EVERYTHING YOU DO

SAM BEASLEY
AND
BJ GALLAGHER

TURNER
PUBLISHING COMPANY

It is not necessary to spend your entire time in prayer and meditation. Rather, seek to make your work a prayer, your believing an act, your living an art. It is then that the object of your faith will be made visible to you. It is then that you shall "kiss the lips of your desire."

—Ernest Holmes, *This Thing Called You*

We dedicate this book to Shakti Gawain—
author, mentor, friend, and singing partner.
RIP Shakti
Your work and your spirit will live on in the many ways
you have influenced and inspired us all.
We are living in the light, thanks to you!

CONTENTS

FOREWORD

I loved reading *Your Life Is Your Prayer*. It made me think, it made me chuckle, and it made me reflect on, not only how I participate in leading our organization, but also how we help our clients as they strive to improve their organizations.

As chief spiritual officer of The Ken Blanchard Companies, each morning I use a voice-to-text feature on my smartphone to leave an email message for every Blanchard associate in the US, Canada, and the UK. I've been sending out these "morning messages" almost every working day for more than twenty years. Why? Because I want to encourage our people to be their best and to remind them of our company's mission and values. I believe that, deep down inside, each of us has a little voice that cries out, "Inspire me! Help me be the best person I can be."

When my wife, Margie, and I cofounded our company in 1979, we had three simple goals: to work with people we loved and cared about, to make a difference in the world, and to have fun. That was our prayer then—and today, forty years later, it still is. Our daily work is focused on driving human worth and effectiveness in the workplace and helping each organization we work with become the employer, provider, investment, and corporate citizen of choice. Our beliefs and values form the foundation upon which we build our careers as individuals and our collective success as a company. Our work is our prayer. How we love one another as coworkers is our prayer of mutual trust and respect. How we serve our clients and customers is our prayer of service and contribution.

Over the years, I've come to realize that all of the spiritual teachers throughout history have shared one profound conviction: human happiness is possible only when the center of the universe is not ourselves. All of these teachers—Jesus, Buddha, Mohammed, Moses, Mahatma Gandhi, Mother Teresa, Yogananda, the Dalai Lama, and Archbishop Tutu, among others—have believed in serving others with kindness, compassion, forgiveness, honesty, hard work, patience, and loyalty. Their prayer is for peace—inner peace as well as world peace. Their prayer is one of love—love for a higher power and love for one another.

In my daily morning messages, I draw on all the great spiritual teachers for wisdom. This book, *Your Life Is Your Prayer,* is your own personal source to draw on for wisdom. It's like having a spiritual advisor right in your pocket—someone who can guide you in dealing with real-life issues: career, money, health, and difficult people and situations. You'll learn how to live the principles of service, how to take action when necessary, and how to face each day mindfully and prayerfully.

I'm a raving fan of BJ Gallagher, her coauthor, Sam Beasley, and this wonderful book. I know that after you read it, you'll be a raving fan, too.

KEN BLANCHARD
Coauthor of *The New One-Minute Manager®*
and *Leading at a Higher Level*

HOW TO USE THIS BOOK

We have lived hard and we have lived easy. Easy is less stressful, less fearful, and less anxious. Easy is more fun, more productive, and more healthful, too. It's prayer that has made our lives easier, so we wrote this book to share what we've learned about living easy by living prayerfully.

Each chapter begins with a couple of short essays or stories, followed by an acrostic or alphabet, then a handful of prayers to adopt or adapt to use as your own. Some prayers are poems, others are prose; some can be sung, others can be chanted. None are set in concrete—they're flexible and adaptable—so take them and use them as you like.

You can use the book in a number of ways:

- You can read it cover-to-cover, if that's your preferred way of devouring books.
- You can open it to any page, and we hope you'll find a few words of wisdom to help you in that moment.
- You can use it as a self-study workbook—doing some writing at the end of each chapter.
- You can use it with a group—with everyone reading each chapter, one at a time, then getting together weekly to discuss your insights, comments, and reactions with one another.
- You can use it as a personal devotional, as part of your daily spiritual reading.

Our book is simply a resource—to be used in whatever you like—in whatever way works for you.

A NOTE ABOUT GOD

How do you speak of the Divine? How do you refer to the Great Unknown? What name do you use when you pray and meditate?

We don't presume to know the real name of God—or if God even has a name. All we know for sure is that there *is* a higher power—the Source of all that is. We see evidence of it all around us. We see God at work in our own lives and in others' lives as well. We see the Creator's fingerprints on everything. We feel the presence of an indwelling God—in our hearts, in our minds, in our souls. That's enough for us. We each have our own personal experience of God—that's all we need to know.

For the purpose of discussion—and since we cannot know the true name of God—we have used a variety of names throughout this book: the Universe, Almighty, Creator, Dearest God, Father, Mother, Goddess, Divine, God, Great Unknown, Heavenly Guide, Higher Power, Holy One, The Great I Am, Highest, All That Is, Joy, Lord, Mighty, Peace, Presence, River of Peace, Sacred Voice, Something, Something I Don't Know, Source, Spirit, The God Which Causes Completion, The Word, Vision, You.

As you read the stories and prayers on the following pages, feel free to use whatever name for God that works for you. If Yahweh or Allah are most relevant to you, that's fine.

Personally, we don't think it matters what name you give to your own higher power—although we realize it may matter a lot to you, our reader. We totally get that. We hope that the variety of appellations for the holy won't be a barrier or hindrance to your experience of the book.

What matters to us is that we explore and discover the myriad forms of prayer in our daily lives—and our relationship with the holy. We invite you to join us.

INTRODUCTION

PRAYING WITH YOUR EYES WIDE OPEN

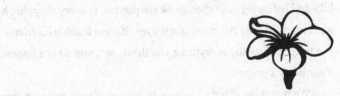

When we talk about prayer, the image that comes to mind for most people is that of one's head bowed, eyes closed, hands clasped, and perhaps kneeling—perhaps not. This is the classic prayerful posture. We turn our attention inward and upward.

Some people stand and pray with arms up-stretched and hands wide open, palms directed heavenward, in a receptive pose—much as a child might reach up to daddy, beseeching him for attention, love, and/or gifts.

And of course, there are those spur-of-the moment prayers one utters in an emergency—in a dangerous situation—finding oneself in a crisis. "God help me!" or simply "Oh God!" we blurt out in our distress.

In less dramatic situations but nonetheless stressful, our prayers are a little longer: "Dearest God, please be with me as I go in for surgery and please guide the surgeon's hand so that I may live another day," or "Heavenly Father, please watch over my daughter as she leaves home and goes off to college."

What we're talking about in *Your Life Is Your Prayer* includes all these types of prayers—and more. Much more. We're talking about virtually everything you do as a prayer. Yes, *everything*. Driving to work is a prayer. Washing the dishes is a prayer. Paying bills and balancing your checkbook are prayers. Grocery shopping is a prayer. Climbing the stairs is a prayer. Having lunch with friends is a prayer. Virtually everything you think, say, and do is a prayer. Your life is a prayer.

We're talking about praying with your eyes wide open—as you move through your day, as you deal with whatever life throws at you, as you interact with your family, friends, neighbors, coworkers, people on social media, drivers and pedestrians you encounter on your way to all the places you go throughout the day. Conversations we have are prayers. Resentments we hold on to and grudges we nurse are prayers. Gossip is a prayer. And so are forgiveness, compassion, and generosity. Everything, virtually *everything* is a prayer.

We wrote this book to help you expand your ideas about prayer and your experience with prayer. Our goal is to help you explore the *power* of prayer—not just with your head bowed, eyes closed, and hands clasped—but also with your eyes wide open, head up, and hands busy with daily tasks. Our book is an invitation to discover all the different ways your life is your prayer. Read it and reap... great results!

CHAPTER 1

YOUR THOUGHTS ARE PRAYERS

Over the years, I have come to realize that the greatest trap in our life is not success, popularity, or power, but self-rejection... As soon as someone accuses me or criticizes me, as soon as I am rejected, left alone, or abandoned, I find myself thinking, "Well, that proves once again that I am a nobody." ...[My dark side says,] I am no good...I deserve to be pushed aside, forgotten, rejected, and abandoned. Self-rejection is the greatest enemy of the spiritual life because it contradicts the sacred voice that calls us the "Beloved." Being the Beloved constitutes the core truth of our existence.

—Henri J. M. Nouwen, Belgian priest, author

Even in Silence, Our Prayers Are Spoken. The Answer Is Yes. What Are We Praying Today?

We may have been taught that the Divine listens to us only when we formally pray—only when *we* say, "Divine One, it's time to listen to me." We forget that English isn't the native tongue of our Source. We forget that we are not in charge of the Great Unknown. (Try telling the Divine. "Stop listening to me!") Our prayers take the form of our thoughts, our feelings, our beliefs, *and* our speaking.

When we come to accept that the answer to all prayer—all thoughts, feelings, beliefs, and speaking—is "Yes," we get a sense of why life goes the way it does. We think it's wonderful and it is wonderful. We believe we'll never have enough, and we never have enough. We say life is hard and we experience it as hard. We feel deprived and we're deprived. We feel abundant and all blessings flow. There is a beautiful song by Lucille K. Olson that says it best: "Our thoughts are prayers and we are always praying."

There are times we wish our love partners magically knew what we want, how to speak to us, what gifts to buy us, how to treat us. We are often disappointed that they aren't mind-readers. But, suppose they were mind-readers. Suppose they were somehow listening, writing it down, and then carrying out our wishes! It would be so easy! We could simply think of what we wanted and they would bring it to us. If we regretted what they heard us thinking, we could acknowledge it and, when called for, apologize. This might be a clear way to think of prayer—that we are being listened to and our thoughts are prayers that are creating our experience.

That might sound a little scary. As far as I can tell, we never need to worry that some Greater Force is listening and is about to strike us down based on our thoughts or speaking. You already know how it feels to think sad, hopeless, resentful, angry, frightening thoughts—at some point you've thought all of them and you survived. I'm certain it wasn't always fun, but I know you survived.

For today, tune in to your unspoken prayers. Assume you are in conversation with the Divine. Are you appreciating life and its bountiful opportunities? Are you living in faith that, with God, you are creating this life and all is well? Are you consciously writing the next hour, next day, next chapter in your life? Are you singing your glorious joy of knowing all is well, that it has always been so? Today, bring your prayer conversation to consciousness and find thoughts that move you toward joy and peace. I will tell you a secret: the answer is "Yes."

As a man thinketh in his heart so is he.

—The Bible

The reason man may become the master of his own destiny is because he has the power to influence his own subconscious mind.

—Napoleon Hill, author of *Think and Grow Rich*

Ready, Set, Decide!

If the Universe gives us a Tool Belt for Life, one of the most important tools hanging from our belt is the power of decision. It's the lever (for some of us, a pry bar) that starts our movement forward toward whatever we choose. The tool doesn't know if our decision is conscious or unconscious; it only recognizes the choice and begins the forward push.

Most tools require practice until we become proficient. You'll find you won't need any more practice with decision—you've already mastered it. We've all mastered it on the job of Life. Take a good look at the life of someone you know well and you'll quickly see a great many decisions they've made. Now step back and view *your* work. Don't dwell on the messes you might have made. Notice how *powerful* you were in making them.

If we need practice at all, it's in making decisions consciously. I've been watching a young man who recently made a decision to be happy. For a year, he had been living a life he had created from an unconscious decision to be unhappy. He recently made his conscious decision to be happy, and now he's full of energy and positive expectations! Now he's grateful for his day-to-day experiences. He's assuming responsibility for the details of his life, and he's doing it with a smile and *excitement* in his voice. I haven't asked him, but I know there came a moment when he consciously declared, "That's enough!" and he made the decision to be happy and to create a life to support that happiness.

It can be hard to grasp the *power* in decision if we haven't let go of victimhood. If we're blaming others for some undesired aspect of life, we can't acknowledge the powerful decision we made to create or to maintain that undesired experience. Our awareness of our power to change disappears. We look at our tool belt and we can't see decision hanging in its loop. We don't even remember what used to hang there.

From unconscious to conscious. From "I *wish* I had that" (a decision to not have it) to "*I am going to create that now.*" Get started. Once you start, you'll begin to recognize the feeling—*you've already mastered the process*. Remember the goal and keep deciding to achieve it. If you stop, decide again. If you stop again, decide again.

You are making a decision in this very moment. What is it?

Get Ready!   **Get set!**   **Decide!**

There are thousands of channels in our consciousness; it is up to us to choose the channel.

—Thich Nhat Hanh, Buddhist monk and author

Attitude Really *Is* Everything

Approachable

Teachable

Tireless

Inspired

Terrifically Optimistic

Upbeat

Determined

Eager to Find Solutions

_____ PRAYER _____

Today I Will Enjoy Life from a Boundless Point of View

Boundless possibility, in my heart of hearts I know that all things are possible, I am as free as my mind can allow. Today I will allow, explore, and experience freedom beyond my wildest dreams. I will stand on the overlook and witness the vast beauty in freedom. I will go forward with the heart of a pioneer.

Today I will greet all thoughts of limitations as gifts—angelic neon signs flashing "Look here! Look here! Beyond this thought is the road to freedom!" Today I will open each closed gate. I will set aside each barricade.

Boundless love! Boundless prosperity! Boundless joy! Today I will see a path of service greater than I have ever known. In my heart of hearts I know all joys are worth allowing.

_____ PRAYER _____

Today I Know I Am Always with My Source

God, when I forget my prayers are answered, I again feel an old familiar feeling of hopelessness. No matter which thoughts I'm using to create this despair—"There's not enough money," "Somebody is using their power to wreck my life," "I'm too busy to live the life

I *really* want"—my under-*lying* message is that "I am a victim of circumstances beyond my control."

How can I release that message, that old story? One deep breath at a time, one moment of understanding that those old messages used to serve me, to protect me, to keep me safe. One moment of gratitude that they are part of what allowed me to survive my journey and arrive at this glorious day. One "Thank you for your service" to those old beliefs. One "Adios, my old companion. Go to God."

In those moments I can breathe. In those moments, returning to the truth turns me toward joy: *I am always with my Source.*

PRAYER

Here and Now I Am Not Alone. Here Is Where and Now Is When I Am Powerful.

God, when we're ready for change, we stop seeing what has been true and begin to see what we want to be true. We may change from constantly *knowing* there is never enough money to picturing paying our bills on time and sensing how good it will feel. When we've lost an important paper in our cluttered office one too many times, we may eventually say "That's enough of that!" with a real understanding we have just declared a new truth into being: that we are now beginning the process of learning how to get and stay organized.

There is great power in admitting what isn't working. From that admission, we can embrace the new. We cannot have the same old thing be true and get new results.

My old thoughts of lack seem as though they are true. They seem to accurately reflect the way it is. As I continue to declare that I am alone and that life is really hopeless, my spirit falls lower and lower. It only takes one simple thought to begin the process of reversing this spiritual slide: *I am not alone. I have never been alone.* My spirit begins to rise like a helium balloon on the loose. It soars!

In this very moment we have the choice and the power to observe and acknowledge what are thinking, feeling, imagining. We can turn to thinking something new and to picturing the ideal, or at least something that's closer to our ideal. We can let those new thoughts and images bring us feelings that feel better and find a glimmer of trust that this small process is the beginning of all that we dream. It doesn't matter if the old picture and those old thoughts and feelings slip back in. Notice it and return to your new thoughts and new vision. *Re-turning* to the picture of the ideal is our part in creation.

My prayer: I am not alone. Here is where and *now* is when I see what I want and know that it is mine. Here is where and *now* is when I'm powerful.

—————————— PRAYER ——————————

The Value of My Life Is Appreciating

Higher Power, like a diamond whose value is appreciating, I'm appreciating the value of my life. Little facets that used to shine unseen—a hug from a friend, a gorgeous sunrise, a beautiful baby—replay in my mind and I experience them over and over. The space of old worrying is filled with new appreciation.

I'm aware of three possible thought tracks:

* Numb to life
* Depreciating through lack of gratitude
* Appreciating at every opportunity

The first two options aren't much fun.

I choose to appreciate at every opportunity! My joy and love of life increase with each passing moment in which I value some piece of this life. My wealth expands!

I make appreciation deposits in my Bank of Peace. This account has a wonderful rate of appreciation! It increases daily. I welcome the compound interest!

I know this moment before me is mine to value.

It waits for me to bring appreciation to it.

CHAPTER 2

YOUR FEELINGS ARE PRAYERS

Feelings come and go like clouds in a windy sky.
Conscious breathing is my anchor.

—Thich Nhat Hanh, Buddhist monk, author

Emotional Weather Report

My feelings are like the weather. They change from day to day, and many times throughout each day. Feelings come and feelings go.

Every morning, I wake up to my feelings. I check in with myself before I even get out of bed. "What's the emotional weather report this morning?" I ask. "Overcast with a chance of tears," on some mornings. On other days, it's: "Sunny and clear. Excellent visibility. Good day for flying." More often than I'd like, my morning weather report is: "Anxiety level high this morning. Chance of clearing later in the day. Tune in throughout the day for updates."

One of the most important things I've learned over the years is that I don't have to DO anything about my emotional weather report—I don't have to ACT on it. Feelings come and go, like clouds. I don't do anything about clouds—other than to take them into account as I choose what to wear, or whether to take an umbrella with me when I leave the house. But I don't control the clouds—I don't try to change them—I don't get upset or yell or assert that there shouldn't be clouds. I just notice them, perhaps put on a sweater, and go about my day.

I begin each day the same way—with a prayer of thanks, with a request for divine guidance, and with an intention to be of service to others. "Checking in this morning, God. Thank you for all the wonderful blessings in my life. I have a roof over my head, food to eat, a car that runs, clothes to wear, and people who love me. Please show me what You would have me do today—what work needs to be done, how I can be of service to others, and who needs my help today. Thank you. Amen."

I often share my feelings with God in my prayers. "I'm feeling pretty anxious this morning, God. I'm worried about money. A couple medical bills have come in and I don't know how I'm going to pay them. But I know that You have always provided for me in the past, so I have no reason to think that You aren't providing for me now—even though I may not see it at this moment. Please soothe my anxiety. Help me remember that You are all-powerful; You are Divine Love; You are Divine Abundance. You take care of the lilies in the field, the sparrows in the sky, and everything in the whole universe. I trust that You are taking care of me, too. Thank you for assuaging my anxiety, for calming my irrational fears, and for wrapping me in your Divine Love today. Amen."

Years ago, a therapist friend told me, "That which is shareable is bearable." It helps to share my feelings with God in prayer. It also helps to share my feelings with trusted friends and/or spiritual advisors. In sharing my feelings with others, I diminish the power of any feelings that seem to be holding me hostage, keeping me from moving forward.

It also helps me to write about my feelings, as it dissipates the intensity of those emotions and helps me get a different perspective on my situation. Writing slows me down, helps my mind stop racing with fearful, anxious, or angry thoughts. I don't want those thoughts and feelings to become my prayer—I want to gently, patiently neutralize those troublesome feelings. So I write. And in writing, I am beginning a new prayer—a prayer of relief, a prayer of compassion, a prayer of forgiveness, a prayer of peace.

> One can be the master of what one does, but never of what one feels.
>
> —**Gustave Flaubert, French novelist**

The Hardest Roads Often Lead to the Best Places

Somewhere I got the idea that if I surrendered to the guidance of the Divine, I'd have only the most wonderful thoughts, experiences, and feelings from that day forward. No sorrow, no doubt, no fear, no resentment—they would all vanish in a moment of surrender. It would be as if my Source narrowed the range of my life and eliminated a huge portion of the human experience spectrum from my life. When I think of it as a narrowing of the spectrum of being human, it doesn't sound as appealing. I almost picture a vacation from my life—for the rest of my life.

I have surrendered, but the whole emotional range is surprisingly still available. No doubt about it, it's wonderful. (Well, no doubt about it at this moment.) There are still moments when I dive back into worry, dread, and hopeless despair. I dive back in, swim around in them a little while, and get out more quickly than I used to. I know those feelings. I'm human. They've always come in and out of my experience. They still do.

There were periods of my life when those feelings were all I knew. I was certain I was abandoned on my road of life—a dead-end road. I was declaring the complete finality of doom. "I will never be healthy." "I will always be poor." "Every time I start to get ahead, something sets me back." On the road of life, I was Wile E. Coyote, but I was certain I was headed for a cliff.

Looking back, I see that same road led me to my life today. I'm on it now, and I live the most glorious life! It's easy to look back. When I revisit that old, painful way of living, I can see the real issue: I didn't know how to look ahead to this wonderful life. I didn't have the skills to hear myself thinking, recognize that the doom existed only in my thoughts, and insert new thoughts of greater possibilities.

My emotions change quickly when I make declarations of limitation. I've discovered that despair is forgetting that I'm loved and guided. Love becomes grief in the moment I declare that specific love is lost. I can bring love back to life when I turn to joyful memories, but so far, it slips back to grief when "reality" returns. Peace and joy turn to worry, sorrow, or anger when my mind decides that there is not enough love, not enough time, not enough money, not enough freedom.

Contentment and serenity disappear in the moment I slip into thoughts of what "should have been true." Something Greater hasn't disappeared—I just forget that the hard road still leads forward. In those times, when it seems so hard, I'm walking around in circles in one hard spot.

I didn't think myself off that road of despair. I didn't have alternative thoughts in my head. What worked was to surround myself with people who thought and spoke with hope, joy, vision, possibility, faith. I surrounded myself with people who were successful in ways that I didn't know how to create. I adopted their thoughts. When I had a mind about half full of healthier thoughts, my mind began to create its own healthy thinking.

In a moment of faith, I surrendered. ("Gave up" might be more accurate.) In moments of surrender, I regained faith. In faith, there is a road map, and on that map it shows that the hard road points forward.

> Emotions come and go and can't be controlled so there's no reason to worry about them. That in the end, people should be judged by their actions since in the end it was actions that defined everyone.
>
> **—Nicholas Sparks, novelist, screenwriter, producer**

How Do You Get Through Tough Times...?

Persist no matter what.

Endure discomfort.

Refuse to give up.

Steadfastly hold onto your beliefs and values.

Envision triumph.

Very consistently keep at it.

Express gratitude for love and support.

Request help from other people.

Enjoy and celebrate every tiny bit of progress!

I Pray I Remember

This morning I woke up alone

Pretending that I'm on my own

Believing I'm fine without you

That you're not at the heart

Of each dream that's come true

So I pray I remember

my heart I surrender to You

I surrender to You

And that I'll quit pretending

your love has an ending

And live life depending on You.

There are so many mornings like this

When I choose my own fears over bliss

Forgetting that I'm in your care—

That Peace is as close as a prayer

So I pray I remember

my heart I surrender to You

I surrender to You

And that I'll quit pretending

your love has an ending

And live life depending on You.

—Sam Beasley

—————————— PRAYER ——————————

Prayer for the Gift of Discernment

Father/Mother/God, please give me the gift of discernment. I ask that you teach me how to distinguish what to do in situations when I've made a commitment but I don't feel like keeping it. Help me to be honest with myself about my motives and feelings. Show me how to recognize resistance—for it does not serve me well.

And please show me how to honor and heed my intuition when it is working as it should—in my best interest. Teach me the warning signals to watch for when I'm about to go down a path that leads away from the kind of life I want to lead. And give me the willingness and ability to be gracious and kind with people—and with myself—when it's best to say "No."

Thank you.

Amen.

—————————— PRAYER ——————————

Creator, bless my eyes that I may see with love.

Bless my mouth that I may speak love.

Bless my heart that I may give and receive love.

Bless my hands that all I touch feels loved.

—Grace Alvarez Sesma, Mexican healer

When I Think, I Pray. My Feelings Show Me If I'm Praying In Fear or Praying In Joy.

Divine, as a child I heard "Santa's always watching" and "God listens when you pray." I grew up thinking Santa was on duty full-time, but *I* told you when to listen. Today I'm always praying.

Moment to moment, I feel my prayers. When I wander away from peace and am worried, sad, anxious, angry, and/or defeated, my prayers say I'm all alone in this life. In peace, my prayers acknowledge the perfection of living. I get to choose from these two different channels of prayer.

Those feelings I used to avoid have become my allies. Moment to moment, they reveal which channel I'm on.

Am I praying my *conscious* prayer?

——— PRAYER ———

I Can Create from Despair or Create from Fulfillment. Today I Choose Fulfillment.

God, I know what it is to create from despair. I know how low "low" feels. In the past I've taken great pride in "rising from the ashes" and creating something new and wonderful.

If I stop listening for guidance, I may experience stronger and stronger reminders to listen! What seems bad gets worse until I've had enough. I admit my thoughts, beliefs, and behaviors keep getting me what I don't want and, if I don't change *something*, it will keep getting worse. On the heels of that admission comes glorious creation.

God, I no longer need that despair to begin the creation process. I've learned to ask "What's next?" when all is well.

"Good" doesn't mean "finished." I'm not finished. "Good" is a wonderful place to start creating the next "Good."

I love my life! So, what's next?

CHAPTER 3

WORRY AND FEAR ARE YOUR PRAYERS

The soul attracts that which it secretly harbors,
that which it loves,
and also that which it fears.
It reaches the height of its cherished aspirations.
It falls to the level of its unchastened desires—
and circumstances are the means by which the soul
receives its own.

—James Allen, author of *As a Man Thinketh*

There Is No Need to Worry Today Unless I Want to Feel Bad and Not Get What I Want.

Worry is:

- an unconscious way to feel bad;
- an unconscious way to lose connection to our Source; and
- an unconscious way to produce results that, when we return to consciousness, we wonder how those results got in our lives. In fact, we assume it's "wrong" that the results *are* in our lives.

Worry does serve a purpose: it defines what we want, *if we take notice*. It defines how to use our thoughts to feel good. If worrying there is not enough feels bad, imagine serene abundance and tell your Source, "That's what I want now!" Consciously appreciate all that you have.

Some of us have accepted as valid the idea that somehow worry is an act of being responsible—as if we're *supposed* to do a certain amount of worrying in life. Here is a secret: You've already completed your worry responsibilities. You met the worry quota. You don't ever have to worry again.

Life is grand. Life is glorious. Always. *Make that your prayer.*

Don't worry about anything; instead, pray about everything; tell God your needs and don't forget to thank him for his answers. If you do this, you will experience God's peace, which is far more wonderful than the human mind can understand. His peace will keep your thoughts and your hearts quiet and at rest...

—Philippians 4, *The Bible*

Divine, Please Lift This Fear from Me and Bring Me Peace

So many of our lives are governed by fears. We don't mean to be frightened, but somehow fear is with us. Sometimes it seems to get triggered by thoughts alone—a perceived threat when there is no actual threat present. We have thoughts that tell us fear is good and thoughts that wish fear would go away. If we knew how to bring ourselves a sense of safety and peace, we would do it. Most of us don't know how.

What can we think, what can we pray instead of those frightening thoughts? Can fear be replaced by evidence of safety? We can check our surroundings to see if there are any present dangers and it might help, and you might have already tried that technique. Would knowing that you didn't create this fear, that it was passed on from your family, make it go away? Maybe a little. Can we check in and see if we're safe right this minute? Yes, and it could bring temporary relief.

One process, and another, and another, could add up to an hour of knowing we are safe. One hour can become two and two hours can become a day. It is possible to find peace one moment at a time. AND we can pray for that peace. We can admit we don't know what to do, and ask the Divine to lift fear from us. If we know the Divine is powerful, we can surrender to that power. We can say:

"I don't know how to do it, so please lift this fear from me. Please bring me peace."

We don't need to know how the Divine will lift this fear. We don't need to know and we don't need to tell the Divine how to do it (remember, we don't know how to do it.) But could the Divine do it? Yes. Yes. Yes. Can we trust that we can ask to have it lifted and that it's likely to be lifted? Yes. It might be lifted a little bit at a time, or in one flash of light—we continue to remind ourselves that we have trust.

In the moment of our asking, the fear will be gone. It may come back, but for that one moment, it will be gone. Sometimes the answer comes in the asking:

**Divine, please lift this fear from me
and bring me peace.**

Worry is a conversation you have with yourself
about things you cannot change.
Prayer is a conversation with God about things He
can change.
—Anonymous

How Do You Become FEARLESS....?

Face the situation

Express your feelings to those you trust

Assess true risks vs. imagined dangers

Regroup if need be...but resist the urge to flee

Listen to others' courage to bolster your own

Evaluate the options available at present

Say prayers asking for guidance

Stand firm in your faith, values, and principles

All of It Is Good

I don't know where this road leads
But I know I'm going
And I know I'll get there someday.
I've been on roads like this and
There's nothing to stop me
And I'm going to sing all the way.

I don't try to guess what's behind the next door—
It's all good, yes, all of it's good.
I'm the last one to know what this life has in store
It's all good, yes, all of it's good!
Every morning's a blessing, a day to be living
A day just like no day I've known.
Every morning I'm singing
"Just show me the way—
I know I won't get there alone."

I don't take for granted the sun's going to shine
And I know I'll be blessed by the rain.
I'm glad that I'm here, won't be sad when I'm gone
But I'm hoping I'll get back again!

I don't ever fear what's behind the next door

It's all good, yes, all of it's good.

It's all good. Yes, all of it's good!

—Sam Beasley

PRAYER

Just for Today

I will live my life thinking of You

Seeking Your advice in all I do

Asking of myself that my life honors You

In all I do and say

Today

Just for today.

I will take the time for my mind to be still

And ask You for the strength

To carry out Your will

I will place one foot down before me

Each step of the way

Today

Just for today.

Just for today

Just for today

I have tried and I can't live my life

Any other way.

All my fears and schemes and worrying

Lead me too far away

So I pray to live my life

Just for today.

—Sam Beasley

——————————— PRAYER ———————————

I Don't Need to Fear the Future. My Job Is to Ask for What I Want Now and to Live In Appreciation and Joy.

Higher Power, I know that the worst that could happen doesn't ever seem to happen. Life happens. When those things I'm certain are the "worst" happen, it becomes clear they are the springboard to the next wonderful piece of life. The "worst" is in my thoughts, and it shows up more often if I am isolating. If I get there, I make the best of it.

I turn my focus to what I want and ask you for it, God. I appreciate all I can and look for the best in the rest. This life is a gift from you. There is nothing to fear.

———————————— PRAYER ————————————

I Am on Track. I've Always Been on Track. There Is Nothing to Worry About.

Higher Power, if I think back to the "worst things that ever happened to me," I remember thinking in those moments that I was abandoned in life, that nothing worked out for me—that familiar language of believing I was alone in this earthbound life. I had somehow gotten off track, onto the wrong path.

Looking back today, I see that those "worst things" were the beginnings of the most powerful changes in my life. From those glorious moments, this wonderful life emerged. I can't imagine how I might have arrived here any other way. From this perspective, those "worst things" were the best things that ever happened to me. They were the path *for me* and I see them now as gifts from you, Higher Power. I can see now that I was on track. I've *always* been on track. There is nothing to worry about!

CHAPTER 4

FAITH IS YOUR PRAYER

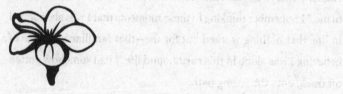

Fear imprisons; faith liberates.

Fear paralyzes; faith empowers.

Fear disheartens; faith encourages.

Fear sickens; faith heals.

Fear makes useless; faith makes serviceable.

—Harry Emerson Fosdick, clergyman, author

You Are on a Journey from Fear to Faith

I'm on a journey from fear to faith. The trip is short and full of familiar obstacles. They're familiar because I make this trip often and, if somewhere along the way I pull a little consciousness out of my luggage, I realize I've seen this road before.

I like the idea of praying for *more* faith, but I already have enough. In consciousness, I know I'm protected, guided, cared for, and safe. In consciousness, I know that all things have always turned out perfectly for me. When I truly *wake up* I see that my risks never were risks. The outcome consistently remains the same: life is wonderful! Even if there is a memory of a time when risk seemed to not turn out well, in faith I can go back and re-think that and say "Maybe I don't see how it turned out well" or "Maybe it's *turning* out well and I can't see a big enough picture yet."

My short journey from fear to faith is my journey from unconscious to conscious, from "lack" to appreciation, from not breathing to inspiration. It's the journey from worry to truth, from forgetting to remembering. I've had a similar experience when I've moved to a new home. In the weeks that follow the move, I'll be out driving and my consciousness will drift away. I'll suddenly wake up and realize I'm driving to my old house. It's an old, familiar, worn groove to a place I decided to not go to anymore. As soon as I remember, I turn toward my chosen home.

It would be great if *more* faith would keep me in consciousness, but I'm a human being and we seem to travel between unconscious and conscious, between fear and faith. I admit I'm not that fond of the trip back—from faith to fear. The trip back is unpleasant and arriving at the destination feels bad, but it doesn't last that long anymore. I used to live a long way away from faith. I appreciate that I've moved so close now. Now the journey is short and quick—as if it takes no time at all.

I live in faith. I leave sometimes. I take a little trip over to visit worry, despair, fear, but I don't stay long. I'll look up at the clock and say, "Is it that late? I need to be going *home*."

Faith is the only known cure for fear.

—Lena K. Sadler, physician, surgeon, author

Faith Is Optional. I Choose to Believe.

I spent the first thirty-seven years of my life absolutely certain I was alone in this life. It didn't occur to me to pray. Someone suggested I try it, and I explained that I wasn't a believer. He replied, "That's okay. Just pretend you are." I didn't know how to do that, but I started spending more time with a few people who embraced faith. The first thing I noticed was that they were happier than me. About two years later, I heard my inner voice speaking to what San Juan de la Cruz called "Something I Don't Know" and I realized that, for the first time, I had a sense of something beyond me.

In the thirty-one years since then, I've found prayer to be useful as a way to be more present in my life and more conscious in my thinking. I've also discovered that I care more about people than I had realized. It started as hearing myself praying for others for some improved conditions in their lives. From that, I realized that I thought they were broken. From that, I realized I thought I was broken. I decided to use prayer to let that thought go and my lifelong sense of brokenness is gone.

I began to notice that every time I prayed from a state of lack, I was declaring myself or my life broken, but I didn't know any other way to pray. Lack was my go-to mode. Every time I noticed that peace had slipped away from me and I was chanting my lack *du jour*, I couldn't think of any alternative thoughts and I realized that, in a state of peace and joy, I had to write a list of peaceful, joyful, encouraging prayer/thoughts. I wrote one list, then another and another, and I carried those lists for years. When peace vanished and I most needed a new way to think, I'd pull my list out and begin to read. Peace, calm, joy, and confidence would return, and I'd put the list back in my wallet for the next time I needed it.

I became more skilled at writing the prayer/thoughts and more skilled at remembering them. When I got my first smartphone, I would pick one or two thoughts and put them in the phone as daily appointments. The phone would chime and I would read, "I'm safe. Things go well for me" or "I'm amazed how my old problems so gently slip away." In time, this process became the norm for me.

Old thinking had been replaced by new thinking, old behaviors by new behaviors, the old life of struggle replaced with a new life of ease. Many times each day I would express my gratitude for those new thoughts and new life. I didn't exactly know where I was directing that gratitude, but I never sensed that it mattered. It mattered that I expressed it.

In my experience, there are four choices that are the norm for many of us:

1. Unconsciously, and in regret, chant what isn't working
2. Learn to think nothing
3. Become conscious and intentional in thinking and choose thoughts that bring you an improved life and chant those thoughts
4. Consciously embrace anger and misery, chant it, feel "right" about it

I notice the fourth example most often in this form: "I know what's right and true and I know you are wrong. You should think what I think." I hear this often, but I notice that it isn't spoken by happy people.

Why do I refer to these thoughts as prayer? Because of the intensity, the clarity that comes with constant repetition, the emotions that accompany them, because they are so often spoken/thought *to* Something, and because they tend to mirror what we are experiencing in our lives. We are unhappy and we are chanting unhappy thoughts. Or vice versa.

Do we have to pray? No. Absolutely no. But! A great many of us are doing it anyway, usually unconsciously, unintentionally, and regretfully chanting thoughts that don't guide us into the life we want. To whom are we chanting those thoughts (or any thoughts)? I don't know. I know WE are listening, whether we want to or not, and I know they are often being said *to* Something and we want that Something to be listening. I also know that we aren't saying to that Something "I want _____ instead. I want to take a new direction in life that leads to _____." If we had that skill, we'd almost certainly be fulfilled, and we might be reading a different book.

If you are having the experience of being unhappy, unfulfilled, or hopeless, your new prayers might seem quite small at first. If it helps, put a salutation in front: "God, I can use a little help thinking new thoughts." "Source, I'm ready to be happy, and I don't know how. I'm open to guidance." The salutation isn't a must, but it might get your attention, and that is important!

There is a pattern I see people take in consciously praying new thoughts:

Phase One: Pray for stuff or the means to stuff (cars, money, a different body, own a home, a boat, to be loved, etc. During this phase I think I was praying to The God Which Causes Completion—I was so tired of never quite reaching what I wanted.)

Phase Two: Beginning to bypass the stuff (the means) and starting to ask for the outcome—happiness, adventure, peace, fulfillment, self-acceptance, esteem.

Phase Three: Prayers for time, for enough, to be in service, for community, to make a difference, prayers of gratitude, and what to do with the stuff from Phase One.

Do we have any responsibility in this? Maybe. The world might be a little better off if we intentionally chanted for what works in community instead of about awful other people. We might be a little more peaceful if we intentionally thought inclusive, compassionate thoughts instead of rage. We might be sitting on a major contribution that we can create if we are chanting possibility and inspiration instead of hopelessness.

Above all else, we get to *choose*! You *will* bring the intensity of prayer, repetition, the emotions that accompany those thoughts to your thinking/chanting. You may find yourself unconsciously or consciously speaking *to* Something—God, Goddess, the Universe, Source, Almighty, All That Is, That Which Causes Completion, and you might notice you hope you are being heard. Conscious or unconscious. Intentional or unintentional. "God, this sucks!" or "Maybe this life can be good!" We get to choose.

> Without faith, nothing is possible.
> With faith, nothing is impossible.
> **—Mary McLeod Bethune, civil rights activist**

Miracles Happen When You're FAITH-FULL

Freedom from Fear

Answered Prayers

Inspired by Grace

Trusting Divine Guidance

Humble Service and Contribution

Freedom from Ego

Unconditional Forgiveness

Learning to Love One Another

Living a Life of Gratitude

——————————— PRAYER ———————————

My Vision Is Calling Me

I have this strong, clear new Vision calling me and I am on my way. All That Is may delay the outcome, but I won't delay the start. Holding back won't get me where I want to go. I know by now that when Vision calls, I'm going easy or I'm going hard, but I'm going. I want to be at peace and have some fun and have a sense of freedom and personal power and feel good about my life. I'm going.

I'm turning all thoughts of barriers, going slow, pleasing others, being smart about this, over to my Source. I'm turning everyone else over to their Source.

I have this strong, clear new Vision calling me and I am on my way. I'm excited about the journey!

——————————— PRAYER ———————————

Only Believe

All that I have, all that I am, all that I give, all I receive
Comes for the Highest, Comes from the Spirit,
Comes from the Mighty
Only believe

All that I think, all that I sing, all that I write, all that I dream
Comes for the Highest, Comes from the Spirit,

Comes from the Mighty

Only believe

Only rejoice, only receive, only release, only believe

All I have felt, all that I've seen, all that I want, all that I need

Comes for the Highest, Comes from the Spirit,

Comes from the Mighty

Only believe

All I have loved, all who've loved me, all I can know, all I can be

Comes for the Highest, Comes from the Spirit,

Comes from the Mighty

Only believe

Only rejoice, only receive, only release, only believe.

—Sam Beasley

———————————— PRAYER ————————————

Any Wind You Send Me

How could I have ever known

The road would lead me here?

Looking back, it's clear:

I could have let go of my fear.

Every wrong turn turned around

And led me right here where I stand.

Maybe that's exactly what was planned.

Any wind you send me—

Any wind will do.

Every day I make a brand new start.

Any joy or sadness, Any peace or madness

Any wind you send me

Sends life into my heart.

I will raise my anchor chain

Stow my charts and pray:

Send a wind to fill my sails

Blow me on my way.

Any wind you send me—

Any wind will do.

Every day I make a brand new start.

Any wind you send me

Blows life into my heart.

—Sam Beasley

———————— PRAYER ————————

More Than I Can Handle

God,

I've been told that

you don't give me

more than I can handle.

But I don't think that's true.

You often give me more than I can handle—
　　so I'll turn to you for help.
That which doesn't kill me
　　makes my faith stronger.

—**BJ Gallagher**

———————————— PRAYER ————————————

Today There Is a Spring in My Step

I am born daily. In that moment of renewal and throughout the day, I choose which pieces of my history to carry forward, and I am burdened by nothing. I do not place the burdens of any yesterday on my shoulders. I have a joyful bounce in my step and I am walking straight and tall.

There is *time* to walk with a Spring in my step—it's more important than anything else I might have to do. Old messages of the pressure of time are released in this moment of revitalization. I am free and Springing along.

Every day I start the day, ready for joy, creating a new and ideal life.

Every day I nourish myself with healthy foods and inspiring thoughts.

Every day I envision my ideal mind, body, and life unfolding.

Every day I go to sleep with gratitude in my heart.

Every day I awaken to excitement and happiness.

Your Life Is Your Prayer

As the flower bursts from the ground with all life before it, I Spring forth and forward. My joy Springs forth and forward. My life Springs forth and forward. There is no heaviness in my step, my body, my heart, my life. I am free and blessed!

Today there is a Spring in my step! I'm floating on joy!

60 —

CHAPTER 5

HOW YOU DEAL WITH CHANGE IS YOUR PRAYER

We must be willing to let go of the life we have planned,
so as to have the life that is waiting for us.

—Joseph Campbell, mythologist, philosopher

Failure...? or Blessing?

Have you ever applied for a job that you really wanted...only to be crushed and disappointed when you didn't get it?

Me too. Dozens of times. I felt frustrated when I didn't get what I wanted. I've been fired and laid off, too. It's painful. It hurt my feelings and made me angry.

I recall when I didn't get a job I wanted at a television network in Los Angeles. I thought I was perfect for the position and was so disappointed when they gave the job to someone else. I pouted for weeks.

A year later, that job—and the entire department—were eliminated.

A couple of years later, I applied for a higher-level position at the university where I was working. The dean gave the job to someone else—someone who wasn't as qualified as I thought I was.

Six months after that, that position was eliminated.

About twenty years ago, a very talented newspaper executive tried to recruit me for a job in Chicago. I was disappointed when I didn't get the job, as I would have loved the opportunity to work with and learn from that executive.

In less than a year, he left Chicago to move to Maine to head up another media company, and not long after that, the Chicago newspaper was sold.

Twenty years ago, the newspaper I worked for in Los Angeles offered me a buyout package as part of their efforts to gradually downsize the company. I was hurt and angry that they didn't value me enough to want to keep me. In fact, I was so angry, that I wrote a book about the company (*A Peacock in the Land of Penguins*).

Fast forward to today: The book I wrote has sold over 350,000 copies and is now published in twenty-three languages worldwide... while my former newspaper employer has gone bankrupt.

The Taoist philosophy teaches that we never really know whether something is bad or good. Misfortune turns out to be a blessing...and a blessing can turn out to be a curse. That's the way life is.

> In order to discover new lands,
> one must be willing to lose sight of the shore for a
> very long time.
> **—Andre Gide, French writer**

LIFE: The Movie

For some of us, it won't be long before we hear the voice of our inner director yelling "cut" and suddenly the stage crew in our mind will be reorganizing the set for the next scene. Did we remember to *consciously* write this next act of life? Did we give ourselves an exciting role in the next part of this unfolding story?

For some of us, the perfection in life is *creating* in eager anticipation and the ideal environment for creation is this perfect life we've formed. We may start by consciously creating an improved life from an undesirable life, but in time we create perfection from perfection.

Sometimes the most perfect life isn't the end, it's a doorway to what's next. Are we so pleased that we forgot that the best story lines have unexpected twists and turns? Have we forgotten to write a great plot change for our character?

How are you progressing on your next script? Are you the lead character in a grand adventure? Do you remember that every change that happens to the star of the movie makes the entire story so interesting? Are you ready for the director to throw in a few surprises?

Don't be afraid to go out on a limb.
That's where the fruit is.

—H. Jackson Browne, musician

How to Deal with CHANGE

Create new possibilities

Harness all your skills, talent, creativity,
and resourcefulness

Accept and acknowledge help from others

Navigate the currents of your shifting emotions

Give yourself credit for how far you've come

Embrace the excitement—and fear—of an
unknown future

——————— PRAYER ———————

I'm Focusing In on What I *Can* Do, Not What I *Can't* Do

God, my mind is a mismatch detector. It always notices what's wrong before it notices what's right.

This isn't a problem except when it comes to trying to make a change in my life. Then, this mismatch detector doesn't serve me very well. I think of all the things holding me back; I imagine all the ways my plans could go awry; I project all the problems with an idea before I even try to make it work. My mind tends to focus on what I *can't* do, rather than what I can.

Don't get me wrong, God. I'm not a negative person—at least I don't think so. I've just got a normal mind that has a negative default position. I suspect everyone's mind is a mismatch detector, too. I notice it in other people.

For today, I'm going to focus my attention on what I *can* do. Perhaps I'll team up with a friend and brainstorm. I'll make a list of the possible actions I can take. I'll focus on things I can control—not things over which I have no control.

If I find myself drifting back into "I can't" thinking, please redirect my thoughts. So, "OK, I see what I can't do, now let's spend some time looking for what I *can* do."

God, training my mind is like training a puppy. With your love and support—with practice and consistency, gentle discipline, redirection of attention, and regular reinforcement, I can retrain my mind to focus on the positive. For today, my prayers will all be positive.

—————————— PRAYER ——————————

I Appreciate My Willingness to Change

All of my future desires will come in alignment with future changes. I will stretch what I think of as possible and create what I've never allowed. I will meet every "I can't" with "Maybe I can." I'll meet every "I won't" with "I'm willing to reconsider" and every "That won't happen" with "I'll ask All That Is. I'm willing to believe it's mine."

Dearest God, all that I'll ever want is in the wide-open future. There is nothing I want that exists in the past. Nothing I desire is in the future impossible. There is no goodness I can create from needing to be right about "I can't" or "I won't."

I'm eager to be whomever I'll need to be to live the life I'll desire.

—————————— PRAYER ——————————

I Am Bound for My Next Focus. My Source Has Cleared the Path.

God, today I know where I am, and I know where I want to be. My old habits immediately begin a list of all that is in my way: *"When you've done this this one thing, then you can be on your way." "As soon as you get this one missing piece and that one missing piece, you can start this new journey."*

Today I ask for faith in moving forward *no matter what.* I choose to trust my Vision in spite of those old familiar phrases that tell me I'm stuck where I am.

God, I ask for faith in moving forward in spite of my old voice saying, "But change is so hard and I'm tired!" "Not again! I was just getting used to this!" I ask for courage to accept that all is well.

Today my Vision is clear and I'm certain to go. *I am bound for my next focus and my Source has cleared the path.* That path begins with a deep breath, a prayer, and a decision. A journey of a thousand miles begins with a single step.

Thank you, God, for guiding me.

———————————— PRAYER ————————————

The Wisdom of No Escape

There are days, God,
    I must admit,
when I just want to pull the covers over my head
and stay in bed.
Life can be hard
and I feel overwhelmed,
    discouraged,
        and tired.

"What's the point?"

    I ask.

"Why go on?

It's just too much to bear."

And sometimes I want to chuck it all,

    move to a cabin in the woods—

away from all the stress and striving,

    my life would be simple and serene.

Or, maybe I'll just run away

    and join the circus,

        like I dreamed as a kid.

Shall I be an acrobat?

    A lion tamer?

    A fire eater or sword swallower?

    Maybe just a goofy clown.

But then I wake up

    from my escape fantasies.

You remind me that my life may be hard sometimes,

    but it's still MY life—

        it's all I've got.

And I'm worth something...

I'm worth getting out of bed for.

I'm worth giving life another shot.

I'm worth the effort,
   the struggle,
   and the pain.

Each day,
   each hour,
   each moment

is a new beginning,
   a new promise,
   a new possibility.

If *I'm* not for me,
   who will be?

It's never too late
   to be what I might have been.
   —BJ Gallagher

CHAPTER 6

YOUR CONVERSATIONS ARE PRAYERS

Words are singularly the most powerful force
available to humanity. We can choose to use this
force constructively with words of encouragement,
or destructively using words of despair. Words have
energy and power with their ability to help,
to heal, to hind, to hurt, to harm, to humiliate,
and to humble.

—Yehuda Berg, Kaballah teacher and author

Who Are You Being in Your Conversations with Others?

Years ago, I had a phone conversation with my friend J. R. and it didn't go well. I had planned in advance what I was going to say— as I knew she was calling me to complain about her love life. So I thought about what I would do in her situation and planned the advice I would give her. But for some reason, my advice went over like a lead balloon. She listened to what I told her, but the affect in her voice was flat and I could tell that the conversation had gone south. We ended the call and I felt lousy. Didn't know where I had gone wrong, but I knew it was a bummer of a conversation—despite my good intentions.

Later that day, I was having a conversation with my son, who is a very wise young man. I told him about my conversation with J. R. "It just didn't go well," I said. "I don't know what happened. What do you think?"

He said, "Who were you being in that conversation?"

"Huh?" I replied. "What do you mean?"

"Well, there's what you were saying—the words you were speaking. But there's also who you were being—your attitude toward your friend. Who were you being? Were you being 'I love you and support you no matter what you do' or were you being 'I know what's good for you so let me tell you how to run your love life?'"

"Oh," I said. "Who do you think I was being?"

"Who do YOU think you were being?" he replied.

"Uh...I guess I was being 'let me tell you how to run your life,'" I said. "I guess I was being arrogant and condescending, thinking that I know what's best for her."

"Yup, pretty much," he said. "That's what it sounds like to me."

I thanked him for his feedback. And I never forgot the lesson he taught me: It's not what I'm saying—it's *who I'm being* that makes all the difference in conversations.

Who are you being in your conversations with your friends? With your family? With your coworkers? With your neighbors? On the phone? In mealtime conversations? On Facebook, Twitter, Instagram, and other social media?

Who are you being in *your* conversations? What's your prayer?

> Think twice before you speak, because your words and influence will plant the seed of either success or failure in the mind of another.
>
> **—Napoleon Hill, author**

Casual Comments Can Have a Big Impact

I recall a wonderful sermon I heard some years ago, by Vic Pentz, a Presbyterian pastor who led a small congregation in Southern California. Vic was a handsome guy, with the sturdy physique of an athlete. The way he tugged and pushed at his collar and shoulder indicated that football may have been one of his sports. But today the sports tale he told was of wrestling.

When Vic was a teenager, he was overweight, not very tall, and felt terrible about his body. (I must admit, I was comforted, and even a little happy, to hear that women aren't the only ones who have body image problems!) He suffered from low self-esteem, which affected his studies, his dating life (or lack thereof), and his overall level of fulfillment in life. He was not a happy camper.

One day, Vic was in the locker room, changing his clothes after wrestling practice and a shower. Around the corner, hidden by a row of lockers, two of the wrestling coaches were talking. Vic couldn't help but overhear what they were saying.

"The guys did good in practice today," the first coach said.

"Yeah, especially Vic," the second coach replied.

"That Vic Pentz, he's as strong as an ox!" the first coach said.

"Yeah, he sure is," the second one replied. Then they continued their conversation about practice and upcoming wrestling matches.

In retelling this story to his congregation many years after the incident, Vic explained how that coach's words changed his life. In an instant, his low self-regard was skyrocketed to unimagined heights because of someone else's faith in him. "That Vic Pentz, he's as strong as an ox" became his new mantra. He shrugged off his self-doubts and set about making those words even truer than before. He worked out with weights; he lost weight almost effortlessly; and his self-esteem was transformed. He went on to become a wrestling champion, while maintaining superb grades. He took good care of his body, took care of his studies, and graduated with honors. He went on to college, then to divinity school, married, started a family, and became a minister.

Those two coaches never knew that Vic was in the locker room, listening to what they were saying. But their words—just ordinary words—had a huge impact on an insecure teenage boy. Their words became Vic's prayer—they changed his life.

Chances are, your words, too, have become someone else's prayer—and you may not even know it. Words are powerful—use them wisely.

> I've learned that people will forget what you said,
> people will forget what you did,
> but people will never forget how you made
> them feel.
> **—Maya Angelou, poet, actress, author**

What Makes for Good Communication?

Clear, simple words

Open minds

Mutual commitment to understand

Mutual commitment to be understood

Unambiguous meaning

Non-judgmental words and tone

Integrity of intention

Congruence of verbal message and body language

Articulate, authentic expression

Timely, appropriate feedback

Intent to listen and learn

Ongoing clarification and re-clarification

Non-defensive attitude

————————— PRAYER —————————

Today I Will Speak from Kindness, Love, and Service

Today, in my actions and in my words, I will deliver a message of kindness, love, and service. I know that my language colors my life. I've felt the love of a stranger in their brief smile and I can smile that same love. I have felt the bond from the simplest act of service. I will carry that bond of love and peace that we share to all acts of serving others.

I will reach across to those I know, those I love, those I've newly met. My hand and heart will lead my voice. My love and joy will pave the path between us, around us.

I know that we are all in this together. I will meet with every being and bring the compassion I keep for myself on my very best days. I have enough to share. I have enough to give.

Today, I will walk with others. I will speak from kindness, love, and service.

————————— PRAYER —————————

Today I Am Speaking the Language of Freedom

I find freedom when I remember my role in creating my life with you, my Source. My spirit lifts when I remember to ask you for what

I need and want and assume my expression of desire is immediately being filled.

I suddenly remember the language of freedom: I acknowledge what's beautiful, inspiring, exciting. I notice how much I appreciate laughter, this cool breeze, my wonderful friends, loving, being loved. I notice my life is filled with the gifts of many previous requests and that I've been asking and receiving for as long as I can remember.

Any thoughts of being bound by
life disappear in the moment I remember:
I ask and you answer, "Yes."

---------------- PRAYER ----------------

Restraint of Pen and Tongue

Dearest God, with your help, I will practice restraint of my pen and tongue today. Please guide my conversations—both verbal and written—so that I may speak with compassion, not with condemnation. It is so easy to criticize and complain—nudge me to compliment and praise instead.

I pray that you'll help me to keep my lips sealed when I want to shoot my mouth off in anger or frustration. Help me to keep my fingers off the keyboard of my computer when I want to fire off a brutal comment on social media. Teach me to cool off before replying to an office memo that infuriates me. Teach me to make the restraint of pen and tongue a daily habit.

Most of all, remind me to catch people doing something right—and acknowledge them for it. Show me how to be an encourager, because the world already has enough critics.

Show me how to support, coach, and be a cheerleader for those who could use some moral support today. Help me notice those who are struggling and give me the right words to brighten their spirits and renew their efforts.

Thank you, God. Amen.

P.S. And while you're at it, I could use a few words of praise today myself. So if you see fit, send a bit of encouragement my way, too. It'll be much appreciated.

CHAPTER 7

HOW YOU SPEND YOUR TIME IS YOUR PRAYER

How to stop time: Kiss.

How to travel in time: Read.

How to escape time: Music.

How to feel time: Write.

How to release time: Breathe.

—Matt Haig, "Reasons to Stay Alive"

What Do I Want in Life? What Do I Want to Do, Be, and Have?

Get a piece of paper and make three columns:

- I want to do...
- I want to be...
- I want to have...

Then list everything you can think of in each of those columns.

Now rank them in order of importance to you, number one being most important, number two being second in importance, and on down the line.

Now look at your list and think about where you spend your time. How much time do you spend pursuing what's most important to you? Does the allocation of your time and energy reflect your deepest desires?

If you find that your time management practices don't match what you say you want in your life, take steps to change how you spend your time on a daily basis. Change your prayer. Stop doing things that don't add value to your life. Start doing things that enrich your life and take you in the direction you want to go.

REMEMBER: Your time is your prayer.

My interest is in the future because I'm going to spend the rest of my life there.

—Charles Kettering, automotive engineer and inventor

I Have Plenty of Time

Your eyes open after a restful night. It's Monday morning, the first day of your workweek. Do you, like so many of us, begin to tell an unhappy story about your time? Does it start something like "I *have* to go to work today...."? Do you tell the story that you're not in charge of your time—that some other named or unnamed person or entity has taken control of your time and is telling you what to do? In those moments, it may be difficult to remember that this mental rant is your prayer about time.

You are not alone. Day after day, so many of us pray an unhappy story of being out of control of time. Our thoughts and spoken words keep chanting, "This is not what I want right now and I'm not happy!" "I'll never get this done." "I never have time to do X."

What about your actions? Are you praying that same prayer through your actions? In your thoughts and speaking, are you praying that you never have time to see your friends and then are you truly not seeing your friends? Are you telling your Divine Source you don't have time to play golf and then proving the point by not playing golf?

We can get very frustrated by what appears to be a lack of time. We spend *time* being frustrated about our lack of time to spend doing that thing we're not doing. Some of us spend more time obsessing about not having time to do something than it would take to do that very thing!

Is there a way out? Yes. Definitely yes. We can each begin to change our prayers. Imagine taking that list called "Things I don't have time to do" and rename it "What I'm going to do next." We can make that same old "can't" list the source of our next actions. If what you want to do has been set aside for too long, set something else aside and do what you want. It can be wonderful to reach a point where you can't do the number-three item on your list of wants—not because you're doing something you don't have as a high priority, but because you're already busy doing the number two item on your list of what you want!

When it comes to healing an old habit of praying for what you don't want, there is nothing so powerful as showing yourself you misunderstood the truth. Show yourself and your Divine Source that there *is* time to have what you want. Show yourself that you can do what you want and that your world still survives. Time spent frustrated can be replaced with time spent fulfilled. Make time to be fulfilled. You're worth it.

Make that your new prayer:

I have time to be fulfilled.
I have time to do what I love.
I have time to do what I want.
I love doing what I love.
I appreciate having time.
I have time!

Time is free, but it's priceless.
You can't own it, but you can use it.
You can't keep it, but you can spend it.
Once you've lost it you can never get it back.

—Harvey MacKay, author, entrepreneur

How to Have the TIME of Your Life...

Track how you spend your time.

Invest time in people and activities you love.

Make conscious choices regarding your time.

Eliminate activities not in alignment with your values
and priorities.

—————————————— PRAYER ——————————————

Today, Make Time My Old Friend. We've Battled Long Enough.

At least for today, time is my loving, giving friend. Yes, I hear this inner clock. Yes, I know it says I'm late, but today time is my friend.

Have you met my friend, Time? He is so kind! He gives me everything I want! He gives me enough.

He says he has my six. He says he's on my side.

I'm letting go of urgency. I'm letting go of emergency. I'm letting go of "late." I'm not just getting there on time, I'm getting there *with* Time. To spare.

> **Today, time is my old friend.**
> **We've battled long enough**
> **And he's never asked to win.**
> **Not even once.**

—————————————— PRAYER ——————————————

I Release All Resentments… Today I Only Have Time to Love

> "Put aside all your resentments
> Get along.
> Put aside all your resentments—

Get along.

Our time's so short here

By the time we start

It's almost gone.

Put aside all your resentments—

Get along."

Today I'm releasing all resentments. I checked my schedule and it's full. No time for resentments. I will check again tomorrow.

Today I only have time to love.

——————— PRAYER ———————

Vanish the Ticking Clock and Fill My Day with Joy

Vanish the ticking clock

There is time to love.

If a timer chimes,

Make it time to sing.

When I am rushing around

Make me rush to serve.

And when I look back in time

May I look back in love.

——————————— PRAYER ———————————

Action Is My Prayer

I believe that positive thinking must be accompanied by positive *doing*,

> and I commit to getting into action.

I believe that action alleviates anxiety,

> and I commit to taking the first step.

I believe that even when we can't do everything, we can always do *something*,

> and I commit to doing whatever I can, wherever and whenever I can.

I believe that little steps can bring about big changes,

> and I commit to putting one foot in front of the other.

I believe that we each create our own future,

> and I commit to being accountable for my choices.

I believe in focusing on what I *can* do, instead of what I *can't* do,

> and I commit to looking for possibilities and opportunities.

I believe that time is my most precious asset,

> and I commit to making the most of each moment, each hour, every day.

I believe that success is about progress, not perfection,

> and I commit to celebrating my accomplishments, no matter how small.

I believe that life is lived in relationships with others,

> and I commit to getting good at getting along.

I believe that true happiness and fulfillment come from
serving others,

and I commit to living my life in service and contribution.

I believe that one person can make a big difference,

and I commit to being that person.

—BJ Gallagher

CHAPTER 8

YOUR WORK IS YOUR PRAYER

Do more than belong—participate.

Do more than care—help.

Do more than believe—practice.

Do more than be fair—be kind.

Do more than forgive—forget.

Do more than dream—work.

—William Arthur Ward, author, editor, and college administrator

The Power of Positive Doing

Shift happens. Good times come and good times go. Tough times come and tough times go. But through it all, you always have something to rely on: your talents, skills, experience, and abilities.

But sometimes, when the going gets tough, we feel worried, scared, angry, resentful, and/or confused. We want to run from life, numb the pain, and hide from reality. These are challenging times, for sure, and we all have plenty to be worried about:

- We have friends and family who are out of work—others who've lost their homes—some whose life savings have been wiped out.
- We are worried about our own jobs, homes, finances. We fret about the future of our children.
- We see shifts and changes—in the job market, in the economy, in politics, and in the stock market. These changes terrify us, and we don't know what to do with our fear and terror.

It's easy to feel anxious or uncertain in a world that's so unpredictable. Even smart leaders are sometimes at a loss. As GE's former CEO Jack Welch has said: *"If you're not confused, you don't know what's going on."*

We experience wave after wave of changing technology: personal music devices, smartphones, iPods, iPads, e-books, and all sorts of iThis and eThat. It's all very exciting—but it can also be confusing and disorienting.

All this change is coming at us faster and faster. The result is what futurist Alvin Toffler called future shock: *"Future shock is the shattering stress and disorientation that we induce in individuals by subjecting them to too much change in too short a time."*

That's a good description of what many people are feeling these days. Just as a war leaves many soldiers in a state of shell-shock, all this change leaves many of us in a state of future shock—confused, anxious, and worried. Some of us feel like *the walking wounded...* or *the working wounded*...or *the what-hit-me wounded*. Even when the change we're experiencing is positive change, it still takes a good amount of emotional energy to respond to the change and not get flattened by it.

Is there anything we can do? How can we take care of careers and our families when times are changing so fast? Sometimes things seem to be looking up and we feel like life is manageable; other times things are discouraging and we sink into despair and hopelessness. How can we best respond to the crazy world we live in? What we can do?

YES, there are steps we can take to hold onto our sanity in the face of the world's difficulties. There are things we can do to take care of ourselves—and our loved ones, too. We can practice the power of positive doing. We can get into action. Action is a prayer.

You can get moving—whether you feel like it or not. On those days when you cannot think yourself into right action, you can always act your way into right thinking. In good times and in bad, you can

Your Work Is Your Prayer

always practice the power of positive *doing*. Like everything else in our lives, it's a prayer.

> Four steps to achievement:
> Plan purposefully.
> Prepare prayerfully.
> Proceed positively.
> Pursue persistently.
> —**William Arthur Ward, scholar, author, editor, pastor, and teacher**

Don't Make Sales Calls. Make Service Calls

Each week I meet with a group of business owners and entrepreneurs—men and women from very different fields who share a common vision of being self-supporting through self-employment. Among the group are doctors, accountants, attorneys, real estate agents, writers, architects, artists, actors, PR agents, personal trainers, professional speakers, headhunters, musicians, construction contractors, literary agents, photographers, landscapers, and more. The topic for this week's meeting was: "What are you doing to keep your business going in these crazy-making economic times?"

Several people said they have upped the number of cold calls they're making; others talked about creative ways they're using social networking to market themselves. Some are revamping their websites and blogs; a few are exploring new business ideas, as they worry that their current businesses might not survive.

When it was my turn to speak, I said, "I've stopped making sales calls. I make service calls instead."

The group looked at me, their faces registering everything from confusion to curiosity to disbelief to disdain. So I explained what I had learned from Chuck Chamberlain.

Chuck was a successful businessman in commercial real estate development (specifically, grocery stores) in Los Angeles. Some years ago, he gave a series of lectures entitled "A New Pair of Glasses" (published in a book by the same title). Recently, I listened to those lectures, now available on CD.

Chuck explained how he became successful...and very wealthy. He said he did not make sales calls—*he made service calls*. He was in the business of helping others be successful in their businesses. When Chuck called on a potential customer, he viewed it as no different from helping a neighbor with a project, visiting a friend in the hospital, or reaching out to help someone struggling with a serious personal problem—*it was an opportunity to be of service.*

"How can I help you?" Chuck would ask. "How's your business doing? What's working? What isn't working? Tell me about your challenges and problems." He would listen with no agenda. He would listen with an open mind and an open heart—with a genuine desire to help the other guy build his business.

If Chuck could help the other guy, he would. If he didn't have the right service to offer, he would do his best to think if he knew anyone who could; then he'd refer the prospective customer to that other person.

In his lecture, Chuck related how, on two or three occasions, he had a different motivation in calling on prospective customers... he was broke, and desperate to make a sale. "Whenever I went on a call feeling like *'I NEED this sale; I HAVE to make some money today; I HAVE to close this deal'*—I came away empty-handed. I never once made a sale that way."

In other words, when Chuck called on people in order to GET something from them, he failed. When he called on people in order to SERVE them, he always got the sale. That was his "secret" to success.

People are smart and intuitive. They can pick up on your energy, and they know when you're trying to get something from them. When people resist sales pitches, it's because they know the real agenda is all about YOU.

And...people also know when your intent is *to help, to be of service, to contribute, to assist them in achieving their goals.* When you approach them with that intent, they welcome you. They trust you...and they give you their business.

I knew exactly what Chuck was talking about. For many years, fear was the co-owner of my business. I ran scared, worried about where my next check was coming from. I did tons of PR, built several websites, chased down leads, and curried favor with important people I thought could help me. I was always strategizing and scheming about how to become rich and famous. When I did get a big chunk of money or land on a national TV show, it made me happy—but not for long. The euphoria wore off quickly and I had to start chasing again—almost like an addiction. What's more, in the chase for fame and fortune, I generated enormous stress, frustration, unhappiness and anxiety for myself...as well as resentment toward those who had what I was chasing. This was a no-win game, for sure.

I always *said* that my work was about service and contribution—and my mission statement said so, too. But it was only partially true. I did want to help others—but I often wanted recognition and money even more. My motives were mixed at best. I ran my business from a place of fear and scarcity...the same place millions of business people are operating from today.

Chuck Chamberlain's "new pair of glasses" reminded me of something I used to know, but had forgotten. The goal of business is to provide products and services that others need and want. The goal of business is to serve and contribute to others' well-being. Money is the happy by-product. Money is one of the ways (but not the only way) we measure how well we're doing. But in our culture today, it's easy to lose sight of the true goal of business and get seduced into pursuing only money. I'm as guilty of this as anyone. Fear makes us chase after what we think will keep us safe. Fear makes us turn money into our god.

When I finally stopped looking for what I could *get* and started looking for what I could *give,* everything changed. The recession didn't go away, but my stress and anxiety did. Money started to flow in, often from unexpected places. I heeded Chuck's example and followed his lead; it made me feel good about my work and optimistic about the future. Chuck taught me to build my business on a foundation of service and contribution. When I do my work well, the result is not just freedom from want...*but also freedom from fear.*

After sharing Chuck's ideas with my business group this week, I began wondering...*What would business be like if everyone made service calls instead of sales calls?* What would happen if business people adopted an attitude of "How can I serve?" instead of "What can I get?" What would Wall Street be like? What would Main Street be like? *What would the world be like?*

He who serves the most, reaps the most.

—Jim Rohn, inspirational speaker

How Do You Spell SUCCESS?

Self-acceptance and self-love

Unlimited happiness and fulfillment

Contribution and service to others

Commitment to personal and professional relationships

Energy and enthusiasm for life

Self-determination

Spiritual growth and serenity

_____ PRAYER _____

Creator of all that is,

I thank you for my work,

I thank you for my life.

I thank you for showing me how to do what I love,

and make it my work in the world,

work that abundantly supports me and many,

many others.

I thank you for the life energy that courses through us,

the gift of life we have all been given.

It is precious beyond words.

—Marc Allen, author, publisher, musician

_____ PRAYER _____

I Am a Laptop in the Hands of God

Many years ago, Mother Teresa said, "I am a little pencil in the hand of a writing God, who is sending a love letter to the world." I hope she doesn't mind that I am borrowing her line—with changes, of course, because writers always have to edit other people's writing. My version: "I am a laptop in the hands of God."

Use me as a channel, dearest God. You are the Source of all wisdom, all love, all creativity, all compassion, all forgiveness. I stand ready to be your faithful scribe. Please give me the words, the ideas, the teachings that you would have me share with others. You are the message—I am just the messenger.

I love the gifts of writing and teaching that you gave me when I was born. My job is to give those gifts away. Please guide me as I use my gifts to serve others, to contribute to the world, and to honor you.

Thank you for calling me to be a writer and teacher.

My prayer: I am a laptop in the hands of God.

————————————— PRAYER —————————————

I'm Done with Hard. Now I Choose "Easy." Thank You for Listening.

Doing what we love seldom feels like "hard" work. It's what we *love* doing! Even if it's hard, it's easy because we love it. On the days we might forget we love it, if we ask ourselves if it's time to let it go, we'll likely hear a resounding "NO!" Doing the work of what we love is the easiest job around.

God, I have done work for money. Tedious work. Dirty work. Boring work. In every moment I focused only on the work, it became hard. In every complaint, I struggled. But, in every moment I remembered how I would use the money, the brightness of the goal dimmed the struggle in the work. In every moment I acknowledged that I love being voluntarily self-supporting, the work turned into the means, not some lifelong burden. I want the life I want. I love funding it and I love living it.

Today I get the choice of asking you, God, for what I love or asking for what I don't want. I get the choice of remembering the goal and having it come easy, or focusing only on my dislike for the work and having it come hard.

Today I remember: I'm done with hard. Now I choose "easy."

CHAPTER 9

YOUR MONEY IS YOUR PRAYER

When it is a question of money, everybody is of the same religion.

—Voltaire, French writer and historian

Mind Over Money

When I was a kid growing up, I received mixed messages about money: "Money is dirty and vulgar," and, "Get as much money as you can!"

I know I'm not alone in hearing these mixed messages about money. Ask a room full of people to tell you what they were taught about money, and their answers will either be very positive OR extremely negative.

I'd venture to guess the same is true for you—what you learned as a kid about money was either positive or negative. Either way, your beliefs and attitudes will largely determine your financial success for the rest of your life—UNLESS you do something to change any negative fears or phobias.

Of course, if you were taught that money is wonderful..."It'll buy you freedom"..."It's a form of creative energy"...then you have no negative mental baggage holding you back. Lucky you! Consider yourself fortunate that the good folks who raised you believed in the good magic of money and shared this belief with you. You've got an advantage over those whose parents taught them that money was a corrupting influence on virtue and character.

Whatever you were taught as a child, it's never too late to discover and discard any limiting beliefs that are holding you back—not just financial beliefs, but beliefs about your talent, skill, intelligence, creativity, and self-esteem. As a therapist friend of mine often says, "Blame your parents for the way you are. Blame yourself if you stay that way."

If you believe that money is the root of all evil, how successful do you suppose you'll be in earning money—or enjoying it? If you worry that you're not going to get your share, how can you ever relax and find peace of mind? If you think that money corrupts artists, how can you hope to support yourself doing your art? In short, your beliefs—both conscious and unconscious—may be making your financial life a lot harder than it should be.

Physicist Albert Einstein said, "A problem cannot be solved at the same level of consciousness that created it." So if you have money problems you want to solve, you must begin by changing your consciousness. You must change your prayer.

> Money is a strange thing. It ranks with love as
> our greatest source of joy, and with death as our
> greatest source of anxiety.
> —Joe Moore, educator

One Dollar in an Envelope

I began using envelopes as a financial planning tool in 1995, after a friend showed me his envelope system. It is not an exaggeration to say that it changed my life—not just financially, but in many other ways as well.

The envelope system is pretty simple, really—you just figure out what you spend every month and create an envelope for each category of spending: housing, utilities, transportation, food, medical, personal care, pet care, dependent care, insurance, entertainment, education, spiritual, debt repayment, taxes, retirement savings, etc.

You also create envelopes for everything you want to have but you're currently not getting—perhaps a dream vacation, a much-loved hobby, a big-ticket item like a new car, home electronics, a piece of expensive jewelry, a creative project, or something else. You write the category on the envelope and also write the dollar amount. Then you fund each of your envelopes.

If you don't have the entire amount to fund all your envelopes, you make sure to put at least one dollar in on a regular basis—weekly or monthly. "Why one dollar?" people often ask me. I suppose it could just as easily be a dime, but I was taught to begin with a dollar, so that's what I've always used. I do think there's a certain emotional power and cultural symbolism in a dollar bill that coins just don't have. But if someone doesn't have a dollar to fund an envelope and only has a dime, by all means, start with that. It's better to start with a dime than not to start at all.

As I think back on my early days of putting dollars in envelopes, I can tell you I learned some very important lessons. For example: I loved fishing, so I began by putting a dollar in an envelope labeled "fishing lures" every month. Then I began to look for fishing lures that were on sale—and I'd find lures on sale for one dollar that previously I had paid five or six dollars for. Then I made a startling discovery: the fish didn't know the lure was on sale! I caught just as many fish using a one-dollar sale lure as I used to catch paying five or six times as much! It was a real eye-opener in terms of the true value of things.

I also liked to golf, so I would fund my golf envelope every month. In the beginning, I only had enough money to play nine holes, not the full eighteen, but I can tell you those nine holes were glorious! I loved them because I had paid for them myself instead of using a credit card and racking up debt.

Now, prior to this, if you had asked me to start by saving one dollar to buy my own fishing lures or rounds of golf, I would thought you were crazy. "One dollar can't buy anything," I would have said. Funny how, when I had no money, I thought a dollar wasn't worth anything—but now that I have money, I think a dollar is worth a lot. Today I even pick up pennies when I see them on the ground because I now understand the value of money—even very small amounts of money.

My envelopes give me a pay-as-you-go way of life. In funding my categories each month, I am making a powerful statement to myself and to the world: "I'm going to take care of myself. I'm not going to depend on MasterCard or Visa to take care of me." My father used to say, "Never use a bank. *Be* a bank instead." That's how I live now—I bankroll my own life.

The envelope system is more than just a financial tool for me— it's a spiritual practice. Writing the category on each envelope is a prayer. Putting a dollar in the envelope says: "I mean it." The dollar is my commitment to myself, and my commitment of faith to my higher power (whom I choose to call God). In putting a dollar in each envelope, I am literally putting my money where my mouth is—I am asking God for what I need and want, and I'm willing to do my part by putting a buck in the game. I am making a contract with God—together we co-create my life.

As soon as I identify something new that I want, I start an envelope. For instance, two things I've noticed create financial havoc for people are funerals that require travel, and pet surgeries. Envelopes labeled "Funeral Travel" and "Pet Surgery" can keep those unscheduled events from becoming a problem, merely by allocating monthly dollars.

I do this with every item, every experience, every life event that I want to be prepared for. This has brought about a dramatic change from the way I used to live prior to learning how to use envelopes in 1995. Before, I would *pretend*—"Oh, I'm sure things will just fall into place somehow. I don't need to plan." It was "magical thinking" that usually left me unprepared, caught without resources when I needed them, and unable to keep my commitments to myself and my family.

Today, instead of believing in magic, I believe in the reality of "works," as in "Faith without works is dead." When I make an envelope and put a dollar inside, I am saying, "This is real. I am making real-life plans and commitments for real-life events."

My wife and I have been doing this for the past twenty-three years. We fund our envelopes on a weekly or monthly basis, depending on what we decide would work best with each category. And I can tell you this: we put in the first dollar, but we've never had to put in the last dollar. In other words, we make our commitment by putting in the first dollar and adding regular amounts of money consistently, and we just keep at it. Then somewhere along the way, somehow, we always get what we were working toward. The item becomes available to us before we ever finish fully funding the envelope. In the beginning, I used to wonder, "Is this envelope system going to work?" But after almost two decades of doing it, I don't wonder anymore—I KNOW it works.

As my wife and I began to fund what we wanted, we began to accrue equity—especially in our house. And when we accrued equity, we left it there—we didn't spend it. We just let it build up. Over time we built up enough equity that we could buy a chain of businesses. Then the businesses built up equity and we left that alone, too. We just let it accrue, like dollars in envelopes. And those businesses have made us a tremendous amount of money.

It all begins by making an envelope for something you want or need and putting a dollar inside. The envelope is your prayer and the dollar is your commitment to your higher power that you're willing to do your part. How does it work? Let's just call it "That which I don't know." Call it God; call it your Higher Power; call it the Universe; call it whatever you like.

I'm so grateful I learned how to put a dollar in an envelope when I was forty-five years old—the past twenty-three years have been incredibly abundant because of this spiritual practice. But it doesn't matter how old *you* are—if you want new financial results in your life, it's never too late to begin.

Today is a glorious day to put a dollar in an envelope! Today is a glorious day to create a little financial peace in your life!

> If a single tool exists that clears the way for vision
> and creates a foundation for having an effective
> relationship with money,
> it is thorough recordkeeping and planning.
> **—Suzanne Lorenz, therapist, coauthor of**
> *Wealth and Well-Being*

Finding Freedom from Financial Fear

ACKNOWLEDGE that God is your source.

BELIEVE that you live in an abundant universe.

COUNT your money and make your money count.

DISTINGUISH between your "needs" and "wants."

EMBRACE spiritual principles to guide
financial decisions.

FREE yourself from negative beliefs about money.

GIVE before you get.

HONESTLY, honesty really IS the best policy.

INVESTIGATE before you invest.

JUGGLE and adjust your financial priorities as
things change.

KISS your paychecks and give thanks.

LISTEN to advisors whose insight and advice have stood
the test of time.

MAKE three spending plans: low-budget, medium-
budget, and high-budget.

NOW live in the spending plan appropriate for your
income today.

OPEN your heart and your wallet to those in need.

PRAY before making financial decisions.

QUESTION your motives when you feel the urge to cheat or lie.

RECOGNIZE that there is plenty of time, money, and love to go around.

SHARE your talents and skills with the world.

TITHE 10 percent of your earnings to spiritual organizations.

UNDERSTAND that money is neither good nor evil—it's simply a tool.

VEER away from deals that are "too good to be true."

WRITE "thank you" on every check you sign.

X-PRESS gratitude for your blessings—often.

YIELD to your generous impulses in all matters.

ZERO IN on what's really important to you.

And remember...*the best things in life aren't things.*

—BJ Gallagher

——————————————— PRAYER ———————————————

Affirmations from "The Wealthy Spirit" by Chellie Campbell

1. People love to give me money!

2. I am rich and wonderful.

3. I am now earning a great big income doing what makes me happy.

4. Something wonderful is happening to me today...I can feel it!

5. All my bills are paid up in full and I still have all this money.

6. My affirmations work for me, whether I believe they will or not.

7. A lot more money is coming into my life. I deserve it and will use it for my good and others'.

8. All my clients pay me and praise me!

9. I am a money magnet!

——————————————— PRAYER ———————————————

Mine Is Mine and I Don't Have to Worry

Today I'll remember that I live under your caring guidance, Higher Power, and that all that is mine is available to me. If what I desire is truly for me, I won't lose it to someone else who mistakenly got it first. You are loving and caring—not a trickster who shows me what I want and then makes it impossible to get.

Today I'll notice the increasing abundance in my life and remember the wonderful manner in which my desires are fulfilled.

My job for today is to appreciate the glory of this life and all that I experience and receive. I will respond to all thoughts of lack with gratitude and remind myself: There is enough.

_____ PRAYER _____

I do wonderful work in wonderful ways
with wonderful people for wonderful pay.

—Marc Allen, author, publisher, musician

_____ PRAYER _____

I Am a Golden Coin. Today I'm Polishing Both Sides.

I am a golden coin—on one side a sheaf of wheat, on the other the rays of glory. My coin is balanced on its edge—I am a spiritual and earthly being. Today I'm polishing both sides of my coin.

My coin isn't finished. I am engraving both sides as I go. I create these images with prayer, meditation, emotions, wonderful physical sensation. I laugh, etch, and polish. I pray, etch, and polish.

I am surrendering to my earthly experience. I have built a strong foundation here. I am honoring my body and my physical experience. I've tried living in deprivation and now I'm choosing prosperity. I am surrendering to the Divine—I am honoring my constant sensing of a greater unknown. I have tried dishonoring both and I don't enjoy the feeling.

In the past I have used fear to lose connection to earth and God—threatening myself with hunger, loneliness, financial desperation, and homelessness. I lost honor for my body and for contact with the Divine. I won't do that again. I find peace and joy in surrendering to fulfilling my physical experience. I eat. I make certain I have beautiful places to live. I have released myself from the bonds of debt. I create prosperity and find freedom in it. I find joy in giving thanks.

I choose my human, earthly experience. When I've tried to overpower my humanness and pretended that I am only thought and spirit, my life became unmanageable. When I surrender my life to the care of my Source, I live a glorious physical experience.

I am willing to provide a high level of care for myself. It is my ticket to soar. The peace I find in the certain, secure, pleasurable, joyful life frees me to seek a Divine experience. In providing food, clothing, shelter, safety, I am polishing my coin today.

**Divine, my hands are in the soil, my voice is laughing,
my eyes are watching the beautiful sunrise,
my heart is filled with appreciation.
Thank Heaven I'm here on Earth!**

CHAPTER 10

YOUR DRIVING IS YOUR PRAYER

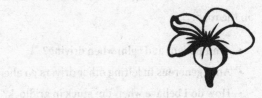

Drive slow and enjoy the scenery.
Drive fast and join the scenery.

—Douglas Horton, clergyman

Driving Dharma

A wise Buddhist master once told me, "When you are considering someone to be your guru or teacher, first go for a ride with him in his car. That will tell you much about whether or not he is the right teacher for you."

I think of his insightful instruction many times when I am on the road:

- Am I patient and calm when driving?
- Am I generous in letting other drivers go ahead of me?
- How do I behave when I'm stuck in gridlock?
- Is my driving sensible and safe, or am I reckless behind the wheel?
- Am I mindful in each moment, paying full attention to the traffic and my driving?
- Above all, am I grateful...for my car which carries me without complaint, for the highways that enable me to travel quickly, for the road maintenance crews who keep my journey smooth and safe, and for the other drivers who are my fellow travelers on life's journey?

I ask myself, *Would anyone choose me to be his or her teacher, based on how I conduct myself behind the wheel?*

British writer and philosopher Mary Wollstonecraft wrote, "Nothing, I am sure, calls forth the faculties so much as being obliged to struggle with the world." Just as physical muscles are developed by lifting heavy weights and doing resistance training, so, too, are intelligence, personality, and character developed by engaging with the world—especially with problems, difficulties, and challenges.

We need look no further than our streets, roads, highways and freeways to encounter myriad problems, difficulties, and challenges—in the form of other drivers!

What is the prayer in your driving?

Do you send a prayer of resentment, impatience, and anger? Is your physical, emotional, and spiritual energy vibrating with road rage? How does your prayer manifest in your day-to-day driving experiences?

Or do you send a prayer of patience, compassion, and understanding? Do you accept other drivers as imperfect human beings doing the best they can in each and every situation? How does your prayer manifest in your day-to-day driving experiences?

Would anyone choose YOU to be his or her teacher, based on your driving prayer?

> Have you ever noticed that anyone driving slower than you is an idiot, and anyone going faster than you is a maniac?
>
> **—George Carlin, comedian**

> We drive into the future using only our rearview mirror.
>
> **—Marshall McLuhan, Canadian philosopher**

Freeway Ballet

Some mornings start out with a feeling that all is definitely not well. It usually starts with thoughts that focus on being late: "I spent too much time with email." "I did it again—I wrote for too long and now I'm late!" "I got spaced out again and watched the news and now I'm late!" I get on the road and almost immediately begin to view each car driving too slowly in front of me as part of a plot to make me late and to generally make my life miserable. I don't think it through, but I'm certain everyone is driving more slowly than usual. I don't know why they would want to so purposefully stop me in my mad speeding, but they do! In the past, that's about when my yelling and swearing would start.

The good news is, it doesn't last. It used to set an unpleasant tone that would color my entire day, but now I notice it within minutes, if not seconds. For the last few years, I've had a little prayer I say when I'm thinking that the driver in front of me is the worst driver who's ever been behind the wheel: "God bless you! You don't need my curses and neither do I." The prayer changes everything. It is a wave of relief and peace that passes through me and I suddenly know that life is just fine.

On the best days, I have a song I sing to completely reverse my thinking that it's "me against them." My song praises our presence together on the highway, and when I sing it I begin to notice that not only is it not me against them, but the other drivers and I are actually in a beautiful freeway ballet. I begin to see the extraordinary grace in our movements. My eyes stop seeing them as hindrances and I begin to see them as dance partners in a high-speed waltz. In just a few moments, we've transformed from enemies in battle to partners in beauty and I'm singing at the top of my lungs.

What a time to gather together!

What a time to be here with you!

What a time to honor this presence!

What a time for being renewed!

As the flow of life continues

And the work of love carries on

What a time for praise!

What a glorious day!

What a time to live!

What a time!

The road is open before us

That we are traveling on.

Each day our journey beginning,

Each day our journey is done.

Today our travels restore us

Rekindle the spirit inside.

Today our purpose remembered:

We're joining our heavenly guide.

What a time!

—Sam Beasley

I sing and move in our freeway fandango and I begin to realize that not only is everything fine, it's divine. I know that I'll either reach my destination on time or that I'll arrive late and discover that it doesn't matter.

My prayers—those thoughts that spin around and around in my mind—can transform the smoothest thoroughfare into a rutted and rocky road. Those prayers can turn road crews, diligently creating a new surface for me to drive on, into enemy combatants. Those prayers can change my dance partners into adversaries. And (thank God!) those prayers can turn around and turn the bumpiest, most crowded road into a joy ride with my friends and allies.

In a few minutes I'll be getting in my car to drive about fifteen miles to my office. Will I notice that it's a brand-new road? As I drive down from the mountains, will I see the extraordinary beauty that surrounds this highway? Will I notice that the cars ahead of me are reminding me that I choose to drive the speed limit? Will I realize those drivers are my friends?

The prayers are mine to choose. If you look in your rearview mirror, I'm the guy singing "What a time for praise! What a glorious day! What a time to live! What a time!"

> The environment you fashion out of your thoughts, your beliefs,
> your ideals, your philosophy is the only climate you will ever live in.
> —Stephen Covey, author

DRIVING Is Your Prayer

Direct your attention and focus on the road.

Reframe frustrations as opportunities to
cultivate patience.

Invite other drivers to go ahead.

Veer away from anger and road rage.

Embody your spiritual values on every leg of
your journey.

What Is Your Driving Prayer? Have You Taken Your Parking Karma in for a Tune-Up Lately?

Prayer to the slow driver ahead of me in the fast lane:

- Thank you for slowing me down! I'm committed to driving as safely as possible and you're reminding me of my commitment. Bless you!

- I trust your speed is the perfect speed for me today. Because of you I am at no risk of getting a speeding ticket. You must be helping the Divine keep me on track to arrive safely!

Prayer to the driver who just took MY (!) parking space right in front of where I was going:

I was absolutely certain that was my parking space, but I know that if it was I would be in it. It is clearly yours.

I was certain it was extremely important that I be parked right now and you've given me the opportunity to remember that, in the big picture, a few minutes here or there won't even be remembered tomorrow. I will get to walk a little now and I do love to move! Thank you!

—————————————— PRAYER ——————————————

I'm on the Road with Friends Today. I Choose to Treat Them Kindly.

Yes, I can scream at you, I've screamed before, but today I'll smile and wave.

Yes, I'm almost certainly going somewhere more important than you are, but today I will gracefully let you slip in front of me.

Yes, I am a better driver than you, but I've made mistakes as well. We are all human.

Yes, I think you should leave this road all to me, but today we are here as friends.

Today I want us both to reach our destinations safely, joyfully, peacefully.

I'm on the road with friends today. I choose to treat them kindly.

—————————————— PRAYER ——————————————

Gridlock

Freeway traffic is like a river—ebbing and flowing, moving along, headed toward its destination. This gridlock is temporary—it'll soon open up and traffic will begin moving again.

The cars and trucks are flowing, flowing, moving, moving, easily and freely. I am moving along with them. We are all flowing on a wonderful current together...heading toward home, heading to work, heading to the shopping center, going to see friends...we are all moving, moving, moving along at a pleasing pace. Not too fast, not too slow, the current is just right.

Traffic is opening up in front of me. We are all beginning to move along. This freeway is like a river, moving along its riverbed. Moving, moving, moving. Yes, yes, yes, we're moving along.

(Repeat as often as necessary.)

CHAPTER 11

WHAT YOU EAT IS YOUR PRAYER

I try to fill the emptiness deep inside me with Cheetos,
but I am still depressed.
Only now my fingers are stained orange. I am blue. And I
am orange.

—Karen Salmansohn, author

It's Not What You're Eating, It's What's Eating You

I went to my local independent bookstore recently. One whole wall was covered with diet books—the Mediterranean Diet, the Atkins Diet, the Beverly Hills Diet, the South Beach Diet, Dean Ornish's diet book, and hundreds more. No lack of information on healthy eating—and how to lose weight.

But guess what was filling the wall facing all these diet books? Cookbooks—rows and rows of cookbooks! I stood in the middle of the aisle and laughed. As I stood there in the bookstore, with rows and rows of both genres on either side of me, I had to laugh.

It seems we are a nation of two minds—we want to eat delicious food AND we want to be slender and fit. We Americans want to have our cake and eat it too—literally.

We know what foods are good for us—veggies, whole grains, fruit, olive oil, low-fat protein sources—but often we don't eat them. Instead, we find ourselves scarfing down fast food, caffeine, sweets, and comfort foods of all kinds.

The food we eat is our prayer. Our problem is that we're praying two different prayers that often conflict with each other: One prayer is for health, vitality, and longevity—and the other prayer is for comfort, soothing, and emotional pain relief.

Food (especially sugar and refined carbs) is a mood-altering drug that millions of people use to deal with the stresses and strains of everyday life. Disappointing love affair? Ice cream will take away the pain. Need a jump-start in the morning? A nice latte with a scone will wake you up with a jolt of caffeine and sugar. Boss driving you crazy at work? Nothing a candy bar or two can't fix. Stressed out by financial worries, family problems, career concerns? Comfort food is guaranteed to take the pain away...for a while. Whether it's fried chicken and gravy, mashed potatoes, a pot pie, grilled cheese sandwich, pie, cake, ice cream, cookies, Twinkies, Cheetos, potato chips, Cheez-Its, candy bars, brownies, mac and cheese, bread and butter, or all of the above, comfort food is what we turn to when the going gets tough.

Using food for comfort is not a uniquely American problem. Most cultures use food for emotional reasons: to celebrate special occasions, to express nurturing and caring, to console in times of grief and loss. Holidays call for special foods; family time involves eating together. Mothers and grandmothers throughout history have used to food to say "I love you" to their kids and grandkids. Food and love are intertwined in millions of families around the world.

What is *your* prayer when you're eating? What is the prayer in each food choice—in each bite?

> Whatever your problem is, the answer is not in the fridge.
>
> **—Karen Salmansohn, author**

Burgers and Fries with a Double Helping of Love

"Miss, can you take my order?" I asked. "I'll have the plate of love and popularity, complete adoration, guaranteed survival, joy, friendship, self-esteem, and peace. And a side of happiness. And for dessert I'd like abundant prosperity. With whipped cream."

Exactly why are we eating? What void are we trying to fill? For so many of us, food gets tangled up with our emotional longings. We don't know what we are seeking or what void we are trying to fill. We just know something is empty and, somewhere along the line, we learned that food can fill it, sort of. Sometimes it's any food. Sometimes it's a specific food; sometimes hot; sometimes cold; sometimes it's pizza; sometimes cherry pie.

We develop a kind of skill of recognizing that we have a specific void that we know we can briefly fill with a specific food, and sometimes we sense that it can be filled with any foods in very great—nauseatingly huge quantities. It's a jumbled mess, but with some clarity and a prayerful crowbar we can pry this entangled knot loose.

A friend of mine—I'll call her Sarah—told me that when she was a very young girl, her father would come home from work raging at 4:30 p.m. and would send her to bed without supper—as punishment for some alleged misbehavior. She was expected to stay in bed until the next morning.

Sarah would eventually fall asleep. Many hours later—after her father had gone to sleep—her mother would sneak into her room with a peanut butter and jelly sandwich and a glass of milk. Her mother would sit with her while she ate, kiss her good night, and lull her back to sleep.

This is Sarah's strongest and only memory left of being loved as a child. Peanut butter and jelly sandwiches are still just as comforting more than sixty years later as they were as a child. Eating anything in bed still brings the same level of comfort as it did back then. She says that she often finds herself wandering into the kitchen at night in her pajamas, standing and looking in the refrigerator for *something—anything—*trying to fill an unidentified longing.

She tells me that she has now passed this behavior on to her children, minus the raging father. As an expression of love, she brings them food in bed, whether they're hungry or not. It's an example of how we learn the emotional language of the family we grew up in—and we pass that emotional language on to the next generation.

Everyone's story is different in the details, but millions of people have similar experiences—longing for food to fill something other than their stomachs—to satisfy something other than physical hunger. For those of us in food-abundant societies, food is our go-to pacifier for a myriad of longings. We seek the quickest comfort we can find—food—and food is everywhere, easily accessible, inexpensive, and socially acceptable.

We can untangle these memory messes and come to understand much of our psychological processes, but there is a wonderful warning about this: "Understanding is the booby prize." When we are all done understanding what is behind our emotion-triggered eating, we will probably still be eating peanut butter and jelly sandwiches in bed unless we develop a whole new set of behaviors and skills.

Outside support, wisdom, new behaviors, and prayer can definitely help. Prayers and intentions can bring clear focus on new goals and behaviors with food.

What are your food prayers? Are you praying for nutrition or praying for comfort? Write them down. There will be moments when you need the clarity. In those moments, your brain won't remember your food prayers, so having them written down on paper or in your phone can be very powerful.

If you happen to be a person who has these entangled relationships with food and you need a new prayer, here is one you can use while you are gaining the clarity to create your own. Use it often and in good health:

Grant me the clarity to seek
food when I'm hungry,
connection when I'm lonely,
sleep when I'm tired,
and Peace when I'm restless.

Food is symbolic of love when words
are inadequate.

—Alan D. Wolfelt, grief counselor, author

Eating Is Your Prayer

ACKNOWLEDGE that food is a blessing—sometimes a mixed blessing.

BUY delicious foods that are health-full, too.

COOK more often.

DON'T put food in your mouth when you have food in your mouth.

EAT six small meals throughout the day, rather than three big ones.

FEED your soul as much as—*or more than*—you feed your stomach.

GIVE yourself a pat on the back every time you make a healthy choice.

HALT...Don't let yourself get too Hungry, Angry, Lonely, or Tired.

INVITE others to tell you what they've learned about healthy eating. Learn from their experiences.

JOIN a healthy eating support group. No one can do it for you, but you can't do it alone. Tap into the power of community.

KEEP BUSY. Boredom and loneliness often lead to eating for comfort instead of health.

LEARN what works for you and what doesn't.

MAKE A PLAN for what you're going to eat each day. You can always adjust your plan later, but without a plan you're liable to drift.

NAVIGATE the perimeter of supermarkets. The real food is along the walls.

OPENLY welcome support and help from others.

PRAY for divine guidance before eating.

QUESTION yourself: "Is my body hungry? Or am I emotionally hungry?"

REBOUND quickly if you fall down on your goals. Just get back up and begin again. Setbacks are normal and natural.

SIT DOWN while you eat.

TELL THE TRUTH about what, when, where, how much, and why you're eating. The truth will set you free (though first it may piss you off).

UNDEREAT. Your stomach is about as big as your fist.
Don't stretch it out by eating too much.

VEER AWAY from slippery places—buffets, office food,
free food.

WITNESS others' healthy lifestyles and emulate them.

X-AMINE food labels for sugars, corn syrups, and fats.
Processed foods are sneaky and food companies
don't have your best interest at heart.

YAWN and go to sleep when you're tired. Don't confuse
fatigue with hunger.

ZING WITH JOY and celebrate every bit of progress, no
matter how small.

—Sam Beasley and BJ Gallagher

——————————— PRAYER ———————————

Carbohydrate Addict

Higher Power, I am powerless over sugar, baked goods, and refined carbs, and my life is unmanageable. But I know that you can restore me to sanity. I pray that you will do for me what I cannot do for myself. Today, I turn my will and my life over to you, trusting that you know what's best for me and that you'll take care of me. Thank you for your unconditional love. I shall listen for your guidance and direction. I shall continue to seek your wisdom. Thy will, not mine, be done.

Amen.

——————————— PRAYER ———————————

Food for the Body, Food for the Mind, Food for the Soul

Father/Mother/God, I know that my food is not only what I eat—it's what I watch, what I listen to, what I read, people I hang out with, things to which I subject my mind and soul. I commit to being mindful of what I put in my body—emotionally, spiritually, physically.

But I also know *myself*—the spirit is willing but the flesh is weak. So I'm asking you to remind me when I forget my commitment, nudge me when I feel like straying from my chosen path, and show me how to forgive myself when I fall short.

I know that YOU love me unconditionally—whether I'm honoring my commitments or not—but I have a hard time forgiving myself sometimes. Please fill my heart with compassion and self-forgiveness when I am hard on myself. Show me how to love myself that same way you love me—unconditionally.

Healthy living is an inside job—I know that. It's not what I'm eating, it's what's eating me. Please show me the way you would have me eat—and live—each day, each hour, each moment. One healthy choice at a time.

I am deeply grateful. Thank you.

_____ PRAYER _____

Finding the Awareness to Know When You're Hungry and, When Not, the Discipline to Not Eat.

I am being freed from the fog of vagueness with food. I'm finding the willingness to be present when food is present. Now I'm able to find structure where none has ever existed. I'm giving up trying to control the uncontrollable and giving in to what works. What I have always tried hasn't worked. Now I welcome real solutions and peace in my relationship with food.

Thank You, God, for this willingness. I'm giving up resistance. I'm giving up the struggle. I will no longer do battle with food and it will no longer be my cloak of comfort.

I'm seeking conscious eating. I am seeking peace. I am finding the awareness to know when I'm hungry and, when I'm not hungry, the willingness to not eat.

My gratitude is boundless!

Spirit:

- Please give me clear understanding of what to put in my body right now that will best serve me.
- Bring me awareness of my nourishment needs.
- Lead me to the willingness to feed myself with the healthiest foods.
- Remind me that water is life.
- Please make broccoli look as good as berry pie.
- Give me strength to stop when I've had enough to be well and strong.
- Give me peace in hunger, peace while dining, and peace in knowing I'm full.

I will find
Gratitude in learning,
Joy in the love of friends,
hunger for inspiration,
satisfaction in self-expression.

I will remember
I have always been well
I will always be well

There is always enough
There will always be enough.

Spirit, please make me as full and satisfied and desirous of the taste of life as I have ever been for the sweetest dessert.

Thank you

CHAPTER 12

SELF-CARE IS YOUR PRAYER

You, yourself, as much as anyone in the entire universe, deserve your love and affection.

—The Buddha

My Body, My Self

Body self-consciousness, body obsession, and body shame seem to be par for the course for most, if not all, American women—and many men, too. Our perfectionism results in body hatred—and that hatred becomes our prayer.

"I'm fat," "I'm ugly," "I'm not desirable," become our mantras that we repeat over and over again, thousands of times, every time we look in the mirror, shop for clothes, or look at other people we think are slender and beautiful. We play the comparison game—judging our bodies by the images we see in the media—and we always lose when we play that game.

The negative judgments about our bodies only increase in frequency and intensity as we age. The older we get, the more we dislike what we see in the mirror. Is it any wonder that millions of Americans are overweight, even obese> Our fat thoughts from our youth have manifested in actual weight gain over the years. Our fat thoughts were our prayers and our prayers were answered in the affirmative—"Yes, you are fat," the Universe concurred. And so we are!

If we want to change our bodies—and the way we feel about our bodies—we must begin at the beginning, with our prayers. If we want our bodies to be different, we must say different prayers:

- I am grateful for how well my body has served me thus far.
- I love that my body is sturdy and reliable, in spite of my neglect in the past.
- My body is luxurious.

- My body has marvelous self-healing abilities when I rest and let it heal any injuries or illnesses.
- Just for today, I am giving my body the high-quality fuel it needs to do its job: water, vitamins and minerals in the food I eat, good fiber, and a healthy balance of protein, carbs, and healthy fats.

> Exercise is a celebration of what you can do,
> not a punishment for what you ate.
> —Anonymous

Self-Care, Self-Worth, and Net Worth

One day, not too long ago, my friend Barbara was watching a popular afternoon talk show on which well-known TV-actress-turned-health-expert Suzanne Sommers was expounding on her elaborate self-care routine: daily meditation, yoga several times a week, frequent Pilates, vegetarian meals of organic produce grown in her own garden, umpteen vitamin and mineral supplements, frequent applications of bio-identical hormone potions, and fabulous sex with her handsome husband. Of course, she was flogging her new book, promising that every woman could look so good at sixty.

Barbara picked up the phone and called me to complain. "Of course she can do all that great healthy stuff," Barbara harrumphed. "She's rich. She has all the time in the world to devote to exercise, meditation, and home-grown veggies in home-cooked meals. She hires personal trainers to come to her home; she can meditate all day long without a care; AND she's got a great husband to manage her career. If I had her money, I'd look that good, too!"

Almost all the women I know are stressed out and stretched to the max, just trying to keep the mortgage paid and utilities on. Many are raising kids—often alone—wondering how they're going to make ends meet. They're worried about keeping their jobs, or finding new ones if they've lost theirs. "How on earth can I find time for exercise—or even sleep—when my life is too busy just trying to hold it all together?" they lament.

Many people believe that good self-care requires money—only the rich have the resources to invest in themselves. Many believe that high net worth is a requisite for a healthy lifestyle. But it's not. Their thinking is understandable, but mistaken.

Here's the real connection between net worth, self-worth, and self-care:

You can enter the Worth Circle at any point. For instance, that famous actress/author I watched on TV probably entered the circle at Net Worth, because she's wealthy. She uses her Net Worth to strengthen her Self-Care, which in turn enhances her Self-Worth. Clearly, this is a woman who feels good about herself.

Now, consider a person who doesn't have a lot of money, but he has lots of moxie, self-confidence, and positive self-regard. He enters the Worth Circle from the triangle point Self-Worth, and then starts taking steps toward better Self-Care. Research shows that by strengthening your Self-Care, you increase the probability of increasing your Net Worth, too.

The third possibility is someone who has little Net Worth and low Self-Worth. She might choose to enter the Worth Circle at the Self-Care point, and by engaging in good habits she can build up her Self-Worth, and in turn, her Net Worth.

That's a great place for most of us to start—Self-Care. You don't have to be rich to go for a walk; you don't have to be wealthy to ride a bike or take a hike; you don't need to have good self-esteem to choose a grilled chicken salad instead of a burger and fries. Everyone can enter the Worth Circle by taking small steps in improving his or her Self-Care. As you take better care of yourself, you will start to feel better about yourself; and as you feel better about yourself, you'll increase your earning potential, too.

You could enter the Worth Circle by focusing on Self-Worth. Engage in esteem-able acts; do things that make you feel good about yourself; practice affirmations and creative visualization.

Do whatever works to build your self-confidence, self-respect, and sense of Self-Worth.

Or, you can enter the Worth Circle by choosing Net Worth as your starting point. Start a new business; learn how money works and make it work for you; invest in promising projects. Assess risks; be smart; invest wisely.

In other words, you can enter the Worth Circle at any point you choose—at any time. No matter where you start, you can begin to strengthen the other two points. *It doesn't matter where you start in the Worth Circle—it just matters that you start.*

Too often, people hope for a high net worth and live in low self-worth. When you make a conscious commitment to learn and develop behaviors that support financial health, your sense of self-worth increases. When your sense of self-worth increases, you more easily increase self-care. If you increase self-care, your sense of self-worth can increase, and your net worth can also increase. When you raise your net worth, you can boost your self-care even more because you can afford it. When you again enhance your self-care, you can raise your net worth even more.

You can enter this Worth Circle at any point and add to all three areas: self-worth, self-care, and net worth. Self-worth, self-care, and net worth are all aspects of prayer. What's your prayer today?

> Your weight can go up or down with your level of self-love.
> If you want to lower your weight, try increasing your self-love.
>
> **—Karen Salmansohn, author**

How to Practice Good Self-Care

AWAKEN each day to your life's purpose and meaning.

BELIEVE in your skills, abilities, and talent.

COUNT your money and make your money count.

DISREGARD the doubters and critics around you.

ENJOY foods that make you feel vibrant and healthy.

FORGIVE those who have hurt you...because forgiving
    them frees *you*.

GIVE yourself credit for having weathered tough times.

HONOR your spiritual beliefs by living them.

INSPIRE others with your compassion and character

JUMP, skip, bend, stretch, run, walk...move your body!

KEEP your sense of humor—even if others have
    lost theirs.

LISTEN to your intuition and heed its wisdom.

MANAGE your time and energy as precious assets.

NEVER GIVE UP on yourself.

OPEN your heart and your wallet to those in need.

PUSH BOUNDARIES and test your limits.

QUESTION self-limiting beliefs and old habits.

REBOUND quickly from disappointments and setbacks.

SURROUND YOURSELF with people (and pets)
    who love you.

TAKE TIME to nourish your body, mind and spirit.

UNDERSTAND that you're perfectly imperfect.

VEER away from negative or toxic influences.

WEAR clothes that make you feel wonderful.

X-PRESS GRATITUDE for the blessings in your life.

YAWN in the face of fear.

ZING WITH JOY each day you're alive!

—BJ Gallagher

What Would Radical Self-Care Look Like for Me Today?

"What would radical self-care look like for you?" my friend Beth asked me today. And I didn't know what to say.

Self-care is such a challenge for me. I was socialized as a nurturer who takes care of others. I always put my mate, my kids, my extended family, my boss, my friends, my neighbors, my community, my church first—while putting myself last. I was taught to be selfless and self-sacrificing—my religion taught me to be a martyr or saint.

Higher Power, I know I give too much. I give my time, talent, energy, attention, love, nurturing, caring, money, space, and everything else I have.

But I can't give what I don't have. I must learn to love myself first, if I hope to love others fully and well. How can I take care of others when I feel depleted, exhausted, running on empty? I can't. And worse, sometimes I feel resentful, angry, and bitter—toward those I love.

Charity begins at home. Show me how to love myself enough to take care of myself *first*. I pray and ask: What would radical self-care look like for *me* today?

——————————— PRAYER ———————————

I'm Always Asking for Guidance. I Will Listen for Answers...and Follow What I Hear.

It used to be that when I tore open a package and discovered something that required assembly, I would ignore the enclosed directions and just dive in. Proving I could do it alone was more important than doing it with ease and precision. But without direction, it was rarely easy and never perfect.

I require assembly. My life requires assembly. The most caring thing I can do is ask for direction from people I trust and respect. And when I receive direction, the most caring thing I can for myself is to follow it.

Today, I no longer need to take credit for figuring it out alone. But even if I could, it's a hollow victory.

On the days I care about myself, I choose to be the student guided by you, the teacher.

I have the heart and humility to be both listener and follower. It's my greatest act of self-care.

My prayer:

I care enough to ask.
I care enough to listen.
I care enough to follow.

Willingness Works

Divine Goddess, Please give me the willingness to do the things I know are good for me. Show me how to develop habits that nurture my body, feed my soul, and cultivate my mind—and give me the motivation to actually DO those things.

I don't know why I'm so resistant and stubborn sometimes—why I continue to indulge in old habits that do not support my well-being. I guess I don't need to know why. I just want to change and I can't seem to make the changes I so desire.

So I ask you to do for me what I cannot do for myself. Show me the way...and give me the willingness to take the first step.

Amen.

_____ PRAYER _____

I close my eyes and see a field of light
and I feel that light and life
in every cell of my body,
nurturing and healing every cell.
And I know that light and life,
and love,
is who and what I am,
now and forever.

—Marc Allen, author, poet, songwriter,
   publisher

CHAPTER 13

YOUR FAMILY IS YOUR PRAYER

If you want to change the world, go home and love
your family.

—Mother Teresa, Catholic nun, humanitarian

The F-Word...FAMILY

Few words generate such a range of emotions as the word "family." For some of us, family evokes warm, fuzzy feelings, happy memories, a sense of security and safety, with mental images right out of a Norman Rockwell painting. For others, family triggers an involuntary shudder, a knot in the pit of the stomach, tension in the neck, with our eyeballs rolling back in our heads.

For better or for worse, your family is what it is. And it's important. It's the world you were born into, with caretakers who did their jobs as best they could—very imperfectly much of the time. You undoubtedly learned a lot from your family *about* family—the good, the bad, and the ugly. Family is where we learn our first lessons about love...and about hate. It is where we see our first role models of what it means to be an adult. We learn about the world, about survival, about money and power, about control and compassion, and so much more. Family is where our learning begins...and the learning never ends. The family you grew up in is your first prayer.

What were your prayers as a child?

> Childhood is the first, inescapable political situation each of us has to negotiate. You are powerless. You are on the wrong side in every respect. Besides that, there's the size thing.
>
> **—June Jordan, poet, novelist, critic**

Blame Is No Longer My Prayer

Have you ever heard someone say something so simple and yet so profound that you were stunned at the truth of her statement? Have you ever experienced a revelation, an epiphany, as the result of a simple bit of human insight or wisdom?

That was my reaction when my mother made this statement to me one day: "Blame your parents for the way you are; blame yourself if you stay that way." At that time I had been complaining a lot about the parenting I had received from my folks. In my opinion, they were too strict, controlling, perfectionist, rigid, and so on. I viewed myself as the helpless victim of their less-than-enlightened parenting practices. I felt that the problems I had as an adult were the direct result of the dysfunctional family in which I grew up...or so I thought. I had plenty of blame to heap upon my mom and dad.

Then one day, in the middle of one of my grievance litanies, my mother turned to me and said simply, "Blame your parents for the way you are; blame yourself if you stay that way." Then she turned back to washing the dishes.

The statement was like a glass of cold water in my face. If I had had my wits about me, I should have said, "Thanks, Mom, I needed that." But I didn't have my wits about me. I was stunned into silence.

Blame—and resentment and rage—had been my prayer for more years than I'd like to admit. It felt like the theme of my life for the first thirty or forty years at least. I look back and wish I hadn't wallowed in anger for so many years, but hey, I guess I had to keep doing it until I was ready to stop.

Mom's simple statement did the trick. It took me a while to come to grips with the enormity of it...I had to digest and reflect upon the implications of her message. But I knew she was right. I could, indeed, blame my parents for the mistakes they had made and the kind of person I grew up to be. Nothing in her statement implied that my parents were not accountable for their actions.

But I also had a choice. I could choose to continue to wallow in victimhood and blame the past for my problems today. I could continue with my prayers of resentment and anger...*or*, I could take responsibility for my future—I could choose a different prayer. I could choose to change.

I always have choices. I can resign myself to the idea that "character is fate." *Or*, I can take the stance that human beings *can* change, and change rather dramatically when they want to.

I chose to change. I adopted my mother's statement as my new mantra. Today, my future is limited only by my own beliefs and my willingness to work on myself. Mom was right...I have only myself to blame if I cling to a prayer that doesn't serve me well.

If it's not one thing, it's your mother.

—Gilda Radner, comedienne

How Do You Find Forgiveness?

Feel your hurt

Open your mind

Release your anger

Give love a chance

Inquire within your heart

Venture into dialogue

Embrace the other person

Nudge yourself to keep at it, even when you don't want to

Enjoy new possibilities and freedom

Seek Divine guidance and help

Savor your new serenity and peace

I Accept My Family Just As They Are...and Just As They Aren't

God, I must confess, there have been plenty of times when I wasn't happy with the family I was born into. These are not the parents I would have chosen for myself. There have been times when I wasn't too wild about others in my family either.

I thought family was supposed to be a place of safety, security, and love—but that wasn't always what I experienced. Sometimes my family felt like a very unsafe place to be. There were times I felt lonely, scared, confused, and desperate for relief or escape.

I know that my parents were deeply flawed human beings—just like everyone else in the world. And I know that I am deeply flawed, too. Sometimes the interaction of deeply flawed folks in my family was volatile—even downright combustible. Man, there were some crazy times!

As a child, I survived as best I could. I took refuge where I found it. And I survived.

Today, I see that the family I was born into was perfectly imperfect. The tough times and painful experiences made me who I am today. As Mary Wollstonecraft said, "Nothing, I am sure, calls for the faculties so much as the being obliged to struggle with the world." My world was my family, and boy, did I struggle!

But I made it through childhood. I have worked through a lot of resentments, disappointments, and anger. I am making peace with the past and finding forgiveness for those who hurt me.

I can see now that I inherited some good stuff along with the bad stuff from my family. In fact, sometimes the things I thought were bad, at the time, turned out to be good in the long run. Blessings are funny that way—sometimes they arrive in disguise and I don't recognize them until later.

For today, I've come to a place of peace with my family. I may not always like them, but I love them. I can accept my family just as they are...and just as they aren't.

———————————————— PRAYER ————————————————

Mother Heart

Out of the dark comes this day
Let it be safe for us
Let us pray into being
A new life
Like no life we've known—
Life full of promises
Life full of quiet grace
Life full of Peace from the start
New life from you,
Mother Heart.

Out of the calm comes a sound
A melody of love
The music surrounds us

Like babies we're held in its arms
Rocked by the soothing voice
Rocked by the loving choir
Cradled in symphonic art
Music from you, Mother Heart.

Out of her breast we are strong
Fed by a voice within
We're longing to hear her
To touch something deep in us all
Guiding us on our way
Leading us through our lives
Keep us from drifting apart
Whispers from you, Mother Heart
From you, Mother Heart.

—Sam Beasley

———————— PRAYER ————————

Divine, I Am Blessed with Love. I Am Blessed with Family. Thank You.

God, I am blessed with a very large and wonderful family. I had eight aunts and uncles on my dad's side and three on my mom's side. I have so many cousins I can't count. I have cousins I've never met and probably never will.

What a joy to be part of a tribe and to watch that tribe grow! It's a joy to hold them all in my heart and to know we are all here. It's a joy to be giving with them, to laugh with them, sing with them, pray with them. Not everyone gets to have such a large family, but I am wealthy with relations.

I am fortunate to have two kind, loving, caring, generous, funny sisters. I am most grateful that we are able to be in support of each other and I am grateful to be their support and not their burden. No matter what, they can never be my burden—they are my sisters and my blood and we are of each other. We are family.

Our tribes are irreplaceable. Those who pass on are never replaced, but babies arrive, and others join in and we grow and thrive and appreciate in value and love and our wealth is abundant. Our memories are long, and our ancestors are cherished. I am grateful every day for this great prosperity.

CHAPTER 14

YOUR FRIENDSHIPS ARE PRAYERS

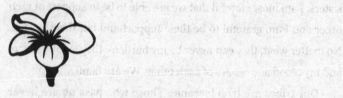

Friends are the family we choose for ourselves.

—Sandra Magsamen, artist

The Greatest Gift You Can Give Someone Is the Gift of the Interested Listener

In my early twenties, I was hired to be an interviewer for a research project being conducted by some professors at the University of Delaware—it was a statewide study on housing for the elderly. My job was to drive around the state and interview old people about their housing. Some of them lived in retirement complexes, some lived in their own homes, some lived with relatives, and a few lived in really unusual places—like the old man who lived in a chicken coop. A woman by the name of Suzanne trained several of us students to be good interviewers. I remember her well, because she taught me one of the most important things I have ever learned.

The training included all the elements you'd think would make good interviewing training: what to tell participants about the research, how to get their permission, how to fill out the interview protocol, keeping track of time, bringing closure to the end of the interview. In addition, we were taught to keep track of our mileage, submit our work on a weekly basis, and participate in analyzing the data, particularly the open-ended questions.

But throughout the training, I had a nagging doubt that kept tugging at the edge of my consciousness. Finally, on the last day of training, I asked Suzanne: "Why will these old people want to talk to us? These questionnaires we have to fill out are pretty long and boring—I doubt that they'll give us the time of day. Why should they?"

Suzanne looked at me and responded simply, "Because the greatest gift you can give someone is the gift of the interested listener." She went on to elaborate: "A lot of these people are lonely—their children don't visit them, many are widowed, they don't have jobs, and they spend a lot of time alone. Most of them will be all too happy to talk to you—you are asking them questions about themselves, about how they live, about their homes and their lifestyles. Do you know how *good* that feels? You're giving them a gift. They will be so grateful that you are there to ask questions and listen to them. You won't have any trouble at all getting these people to talk to you."

Suzanne was so right. But she wasn't just right about old people—she was right about *all* people. Think about it. What is it we all want more than anything? We want to be *heard*, to be acknowledged, to have someone validate our existence and our thoughts and feelings. I have tested this out in many, many ways. I practice good listening skills with my friends, and they know that I love them. I listen to the men that I date, and they think I'm charming and delightful. I listen to participants in the seminars that I teach, and they think that I'm brilliant. I listen to my neighbors, and they think I'm a good problem solver. All I'm doing is providing a witness—a type of listening that conveys a message: "You're important. I care about what you think—that's why I'm listening."

When I think about all the friends I have, which ones do I like the most? The ones who listen to me best.

In return, I try to be a good listener myself, in order to build and strengthen our friendship. Listening is my prayer.

Like a bank account, friendships grow in direct
proportion of interest paid.

—Peter McWilliams, poet

I Allow My Friends the Dignity of Their Choices

Teri was in tears at our weekly support group meeting. At age forty-four, she was undergoing fertility treatments, trying to get pregnant. Just a couple years earlier, she had been focused intensely on her quest to find a husband. Having accomplished that and married him a few months ago, she was now on an equally intense quest to get pregnant. So far, no luck.

The fertility treatments required that she give herself daily hormone shots, and, being afraid of needles, she was freaking out. Not only that, the changes in her hormone levels were making her crazy. She was putting herself through so much stress that I wondered aloud if it was worth it. "Did you consider the possibility that maybe God doesn't want you to have a baby?" I asked gently after our meeting was over and we were alone.

The look of horror and disbelief on her face told me I had made a major blunder. I apologized instantly. "I'm so sorry. I shouldn't have said anything. It's none of my business," I said, backpedaling as fast as I could. But it was too late—the damage was done.

Before I got home from the meeting, Teri had left a voicemail message telling me how hurt she was, how inappropriate my comment was, and how disappointed she was that I was so un-supportive of her quest for motherhood. My intention had been good, but the impact had been bad. What could I do?

I had a long conversation with Marcia, another member of our support group. I told her of my faux pas. She listened sympathetically, saying she understood my kind intentions. I was simply trying to save Teri more months of heartache by suggesting that perhaps she was on a path that was not right for her. I didn't *tell* her she was making a mistake—I simply inquired, raising the possibility for her to consider.

But Marcia also pointed out that it really was none of my business. It's one thing if you see a friend doing something that will endanger her health or her life—like driving drunk, or using hard drugs, or staying with an abusive husband. But trying to get pregnant is not a life-threatening activity—it's a personal choice. Marcia pointed out to me that "We need to allow other people the dignity of their own choices."

She was so right, and I am forever grateful for her succinct wisdom. Some lessons in life I have had to learn through stupid mistakes—and this was one of them! Teri has since forgiven me, and we have continued our friendship.

Most importantly, I have learned the importance of refraining from giving unsolicited advice. Whether someone is my friend or a stranger, what they do with their personal lives is none of my business—unless it affects me (and even then, I should speak up only after careful thought and reflection).

"The dignity of personal choice"—what a wonderful concept!—the essence of free will and self-determination. I certainly want it myself. I must allow others have it too.

My prayer today: I allow my friends the dignity of their own choices.

> No love, no friendship can cross the path of our
> destiny without leaving some mark on it forever.
> **—Janeen Koconis, graphic artist**

Friendship Promise

I believe that true friends accept each other just as they are,
    and I promise to love you unconditionally.

I believe that true friends listen with their hearts as well as their ears,
    and I promise to give you my attention and affection.

I believe that true friends keep each other's confidences,
    and I promise to be trustworthy and loyal.

I believe that true friends complement each other,
    and I promise to celebrate our individuality, as well as all we share in common.

I believe that true friends complement each other,

and I promise to acknowledge your many unique qualities—

especially when you forget how wonderful you are.

I believe that true friends enjoy their sense of humor,

and I promise to laugh with you, not at you.

I believe that true friends rely on each other in good times and bad,

and I promise to be there for you.

I believe that true friends are honest with each other,

and I promise to tell you the truth with love.

I believe that true friends forgive each other's mistakes and failings,

and I promise to let go of disappointments and resentments.

I believe that true friends share generously,

and I promise to open my heart and my home to you.

I believe that true friends love spending time together,

and I promise to make time for you.

I believe that true friends cherish each other,

and I promise to honor your feelings.

I believe that true friends allow each other the dignity of their own choices,

and I promise to respect and support you in your decisions.

I believe that true friends give each other the freedom to be who they are,

and I promise to love you for being *you*.

—BJ Gallagher

_____ PRAYER _____

Help!

Divine, I've heard that "a friend in need is a friend indeed." Today, my friend is in need and I don't know how to help her, so I'm asking you.

Her pain is so great and I feel powerless to help her. There is nothing I can do take her pain away, though I want to more than anything.

But perhaps there is something I do to ease her pain somewhat. Please guide me, Divine, and show me how I might help my friend.

And please hold her in your loving arms—comfort her, soother her, reassure you of your unwavering care. She is your daughter and I know you love her, as you love all your children.

Thank you.

Amen.

_____ PRAYER _____

Whole

I will clear my vision
And look at you anew
With love in my heart.
I'll search through my days
And I will find healing
For each wounded part

Until my eyes are free to

See us both as whole.

Father, Mother, God

Spirit of my soul

Look through your eyes and see me

Whole, whole, whole.

Every broken friend

Every shattered soul

Healed in the eyes that see me

Whole, Whole, Whole.

Healed in the eyes that see me whole.

—Sam Beasley

—————————— PRAYER ——————————

God's Apology

God, some say that "friends are God's apology for your family."

If that's true, apology accepted.

The friends you've brought into my life are amazing—kind, thoughtful, generous, smart, interesting, talented, creative, compassionate, tolerant, and forgiving—truly wonderful human beings. Some of them are funny, too. That's a bonus—I love people who can make me laugh.

So thank you, God. You know I'm not too wild about the family I was born into—I have talked to you about them many times over the years. But you totally made up for it with all the friends you've given me.

Thank you!

—————————— PRAYER ——————————

In the Love of Friends I Sense the Great Love

Now that I have everything, I realize I only have loving companions. Nothing else matters. Wrapped in the embrace of friends, all else vanishes.

Looking back, I realize that if I had worked as hard to befriend others as I have to gain riches, I would now know and be friends with everyone on earth. Every morning and every evening I write a list of my gratefulness. It's almost always a list of my love for friends. Other wealth seldom makes the list.

Today I will cherish the embrace of love. Today I will give thanks for the presence of the Divine in the faces of my friends. My wealth is measured in love. In that love,

I sense the Great Love.

CHAPTER 15

RELATIONSHIPS AND COMMUNITY ARE YOUR PRAYERS

The deepest need of man is the need to overcome his separateness, to leave the prison of his aloneness.

—Erich Fromm, therapist, author

Other People

"Hell is other people," wrote the French existential philosopher, Jean-Paul Sartre. He was right, but only half right. The other half is, "Heaven is other people, too." Yes, it is our relationships with other people that give us most of our headaches—but relationships can also give us much joy.

Bankers can be overheard muttering, "This would be a great place to work, if it weren't for the customers." University people sometimes comment, "This would be a great place, if it weren't for the students." Record company executives love the music industry—but complain that the musicians are a pain in the ass. Book publishers occasionally gripe, "This would be a wonderful business, if only we didn't have to deal with pesky authors." In every workplace, there are troublesome people. Employees bitch about their bosses; bosses complain about their employees. Departments point the finger at each other. And customers blame everyone.

So you go home at the end of the day, hoping to find a little peace, quiet, understanding, love, and support. And what do you get? Whining kids, sulking teens, and/or a spouse who's had his or her own share of difficult people to deal with today.

Difficult people are everywhere—in neighborhoods, schools, hospitals, government, and yes, even in churches, temples, ashrams, monasteries, and mosques. And isn't it funny how everyone seems to think that *someone else* is the problem?

What are we to do? We can't seem to live with one another, but we can't live without one another.

Woody Allen summarized our predicament at the end of his movie *Annie Hall* when he turned to the camera and said:

> I was complaining to my shrink the other day that my brother is driving me crazy—he thinks he's a chicken.
> My shrink said, "Well, then, just stay away from him. If it bothers you so much, just avoid him."
> "I'd like to," I replied, "but I need the eggs."

That's our dilemma: How do we live in community with other people? How can we live and work together, getting the "eggs" we need without hurting each other? How do we accomplish this difficult goal...without having to walk on eggshells?

What are your prayers about "other people"?

> I have learned silence from the talkative,
> toleration from the intolerant,
> and kindness from the unkind;
> yet, strange, I am ungrateful to those teachers.
> **—Kahlil Gibran, Lebanese-American author**

Heaven and Hell

Some years ago, author and psychiatrist M. Scott Peck gave a lecture in which he asserted that the biblical phrase "the Kingdom of God is within you" has been mistranslated and misunderstood throughout history. Dr. Peck said that if you go back to the original Aramaic, in which that piece of Scripture is written, what it actually says is: "The Kingdom of God is AMONG you." That is, the Kingdom of God is in *community*. Wherever two or more are gathered, God is there.

Peck's comments reminded me of an ancient allegory about Heaven and Hell:

A holy man was having a conversation with the Lord one day and said, "Lord, I would like to know what Heaven and Hell are like."

The Lord led the holy man to two doors. He opened one for the holy man to peer inside. In the middle of the room was a large round table, in the middle of which was a huge pot of stew that smelled delicious. But the people sitting around the table were emaciated, pale, and sickly. They appeared to be famished. They all had spoons with very long handles splinted to their arms, but each found it impossible to reach into the pot of stew and take a spoonful because they could not get the long-handled spoons to their mouths. The holy man shuddered at the sight of their misery and suffering. The Lord said, "You have seen Hell."

The Lord took the holy man to the next room and opened the door. It was exactly the same as the first one, with a large round table, in the middle of which was a huge pot of stew that smelled delicious. The people's arms were splinted with the same long-handled spoons as in the other room, but in this room, the people were well-nourished and healthy. They were all laughing and talking, as they took turns scooping up big spoonfuls of stew and then feeding each other.

Your Life Is Your Prayer

The holy man turned to the Lord and said, "Oh, now I see the difference."

"Yes," said the Lord, "Here in Heaven, people have learned to feed each other...while in Hell, people think only of themselves."

> Alone we can do so little; together we can do
> so much.
>
> **—Helen Keller, deaf/blind author, lecturer**

What is COMMUNITY?

Coming together

Open arms, open minds, open hearts

Mutual respect

Mutual support

Understanding differences

Never losing sight of common goals

Integrity—both individual and collective

Trust and truth

"Yes!" to healthy interdependence

No One Can Do It for Me, But I Can't Do It Alone

Higher Power, I know that self-reliance is one of my strengths, but it's also my most serious weakness. So often I feel frustrated, isolated, and exhausted from trying to go it alone.

I know that in American society, we tend to over-value the individual and under-value community. We wholeheartedly subscribe to the myth of the rugged individual—John Wayne, the Lone Ranger, the strong silent type. And we often fail to appreciate that fact that there is ample research and evidence to prove that we all do better when we team up with others.

I know that's true for me. I come from a family of Lone Rangers. Self-sufficiency was drilled into me from a very young age.

Years ago, I read that a Clydesdale horse can pull five thousand pounds by himself. But two Clydesdales have pulling power that is *five times* the pulling capacity of one horse. The synergy between the two horses increases their work capacity exponentially.

And so it is with people, too. Together we are greater than the sum of our parts. Two heads really are better than one, especially if the two heads are smart enough to know that they're more creative and productive together.

God, I know that you designed us humans to live and work in relationship with one another—in pairs, in partnerships, in groups, in teams, in families, in associations, in neighborhoods, in organizations, in clans and communities of all sizes and types.

Please remind me to reach out and ask for help, to let others support me. Help me learn from them, and lean on them when I need to. I know I am responsible for my own life and my own success, but I don't have to do it all by myself.

--- PRAYER ---

Divine Love, Thank You for this Community of Love

I love people! Everywhere I go I find people who are so kind and funny and loving. I gather people who want to get together and sing, and the world is full of people who want to sing. Everywhere I go I find people who want to gather for dinner and gather to be in service and support and love.

When I had been alone long enough, I realized that communities begin in invitation. I took a breath and became the inviter. It is the greatest gift I have—so many wonderful people are waiting to be invited and are so happy to say "Yes." If I could give you anything, I'd give you the great prosperity that comes to those who invite and those who accept that invitation.

It is easy to be alone. Our world is set up to support aloneness. We could almost not notice that we are a community of friends who haven't met. But we *are* a community and we aren't loners and the blessing of friends is beyond magical.

I saw a video of a man on a crowded subway car who passed out lyrics to a song. He didn't outright invite them to sing, he just began to sing and the other riders—all strangers—began to sing with him. Before the song was finished, they were smiling. They had a bond. They had been a car full of strangers, each alone, and they became a community in less than the length of one song. That is who we are, strangers alone waiting to be invited to join in community. We are called to belong.

We are beautiful!

Thank you for this community of love!

Thank you!

———————— PRAYER ————————

Those Who Deserve Love Least, Need It the Most

Dearest God, many years ago, I saw a church marquee in North Carolina that read: "Those who deserve love least, need it the most." It stopped me in my tracks. What a concept! It was not a message I was particularly happy to receive.

But I knew it was an important message. And I knew it was for me.

It is so easy to love people who are loveable, those who are nice, those who are pleasant, those who are kind and generous. It's hard to love the jerks and assholes of the world.

But I know I must give it my best shot. For You love me unconditionally—even when I'm being a jerk or an asshole—and so I am called to love my fellow human beings just as you love me. It even says so in one of your Ten Commandments (though I must confess I can't remember which one).

So, God, I shall do my best to love those who deserve it the least. In all honesty, I don't want to love them. I want to avoid them, judge them, condemn them, ostracize them, and punish them. But if I am to love my fellow humans the way that you love me—unconditionally—then I will rise to the challenge today and do my very best.

God, give me strength!

CHAPTER 16

YOUR MUSIC, BOOKS, MOVIES, AND ART ARE PRAYERS

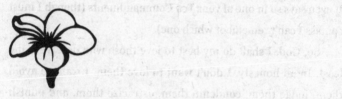

The goal of life is rapture.
Art is the way we experience it.
Art is the transforming experience.

—Joseph Campbell, mythologist

A Prayer of Beauty

I'm married to a professional photographer. I have always liked the art of photography, though I am not a photographer. I've always loved seeing a deeper, richer world in photographs than my eyes might have seen in passing over the exact scene in the photograph. My wife, Suzanne, uses the term "wabi sabi." She finds beauty in the imperfect, the impermanent, that which is disappearing. Until I saw the beauty that she brings to a photograph of an old metal door or fire hydrant, all I saw was rust. Her photos give me new eyes.

A powerful photograph is like a novel to me. I can see an entire world in a photograph. I know the stories. I know the characters. I know why the front fender is dented in an old truck in a photo. I step into that world.

Art that we love can bring such pleasure, such vast experiences! Our emotional range stretches to include the emotions in the book, painting, photograph. The artist creates a world—captures it in time and space and we get to travel in that world. We have a role there: we are the curious detectives, anticipating the next page in the book or the next scene in a never-changing photo.

We open a book and come to know the characters. Some of them become such good friends, it's hard to believe we can't have them over for dinner. In historical novels and biographies, we come to know people who've had a profound effect on our lives, though they may have been dead for years.

Our favorite artists create worlds in which we love to travel. We experience one of their worlds and long for the next. We wait to safely become an intimate part of those next worlds.

We get cozy and warm in our beds. We open to page one of a new world, a new universe. We envision the first scene and we are off and away. We are travelers and our beds can fly.

> Every artist dips his brush in his own soul
> and paints his own nature into his pictures.
>
> **—Henry Ward Beecher, clergyman, social
> reformer**

Music Touches My Soul

Some years ago, my friend Nell and I were talking about local churches, as I had been searching for a spiritual home but hadn't found it yet. "Try that church in Old Town, Pasadena," Nell said.

"I've tried that church a couple times in the past, but didn't like the pastor's style," I replied. "Too much ego, methinks."

"That pastor retired and they have a new pastor now," Nell said. "You should check it out. I really think you'll like the new guy."

So I took Nell's suggestion and went to that church one Sunday. The new preacher was good. Down to earth, accessible, and likeable. But what made a bigger impression on me was the music. When the choir sang and when the congregation sang, I cried.

"Must be tired," I told myself. "It's just a one-time thing. I'll come back next week and it'll be different."

I did go back the following week...and once again, the music moved me to tears. The organ, the voices lifting together in praise and worship, touched my heart and moved my spirit in ways no spoken words did.

I went back to church for a third time and sure enough, the same thing happened. I cried every time the music played and people sang.

I knew I had found my spiritual home. The minister was good; the sanctuary was beautiful; the parishioners were warm and friendly; but what fed my soul was the music.

Music is one of the most powerful prayers there is. What are the music prayers you choose to listen to throughout your day? What is the song you sing in your heart?

Today, try singing your prayers!

Where words fail, music speaks.

—**Hans Christian Anderson, Dutch author.**

If I should ever die, God forbid, let this be my epitaph: "The only proof he needed for the existence of God was music."

—**Kurt Vonnegut, author**

How to Be More Creative

ALLOW yourself to make "bad" art before you make "good" art. Creativity is a process, and in the end, it's all good.

BREATHE! To breathe is to in-spire. Breathe creativity. In-spire.

CREATE generously. Your creativity is a gift you give to the world.

DREAM...and become the student of your dreams.

ELEVATE your creativity in importance in your daily priorities.

FUND YOUR ART. Don't wait for your art to fund your life.

GROW creatively. Try out what you've never tried.

HEED little glimmers of vision; attention to glimmers is like water to flowers.

INVITE the Divine Creativity into your hands, heart, and mind.

JUDGE later. Create now. Creating and judging come
   from different parts of the brain.

KNOW that your creations are meaningful and
   important, even if you don't know how or why.

LEARN from artists who inspire you.

MAKE TIME for art—to see it, to listen to it, to feel it, to
   create it.

NAVIGATE the sea of emotions while you're creating.
   Buckle up. It might be a bumpy ride.

OPEN your heart and mind to inspiration.

PRACTICE DIVERGENT THINKING. Exercise your
   creativity by asking, "What are all the possible ways
   to solve this problem?"

QUESTION the critic in your mind. Don't believe
   everything you think.

RESPECT others' creativity, too.

SAVE your creative works even if you don't use them
   today. Things can be recycled and up-cycled in
   the future.

TREAT feedback as a gift—the good, the bad, and
 yes, even the ugly. Feedback is the breakfast
 of champions.

UNDERSTAND that not everyone will like your art.
 That's OK. You won't like everyone else's art either.

VALUE your art and the time you spent creating it.

WELCOME each inspiration...even if it seems
 weird at first.

X-PRESS YOUR CREATIVITY in all aspects of your life.

YODEL, or sing, or hum, or whistle while you work.

ZING WITH JOY whenever you feel the urge to create!

—Sam Beasley and BJ Gallagher

_____ PRAYER _____

I Gain the Freedom to Peacefully Create from the Foundation of What's True.

What's in my life has already been created. Thank you, God. If I want more of it, I will consciously appreciate it. This certain trueness of my life frees me to dream.

Thank you for my food, shelter, safety, friendship, love, meaningful work, artistic freedom. I have boundless appreciation for these qualities of life and no fear of loss. My life is stable. There is no need for last-minute bail-outs, no "just in the nick of time."

Today I pray to be open to my next creative inspiration. I'm looking forward to its arrival! I'm free to invite in possibilities I've never allowed into my dreaming. I'm free to play. I'm free to create. I'm free to serve.

My needs are taken care of and they form a strong and stable foundation. From that foundation, I am free. From that foundation, I leap into the glorious unknown.

_____ PRAYER _____

From the Heart

There's a road out before me, I can't see 'round the bend
I don't know where I'm going, I don't know where it ends

I know I've got to get there
I don't know how I'm ever gonna start.

I'm reaching here inside me and
I hope I'm gonna get it
From the heart, from the heart,
From the heart.

Call on me Spirit, tell me what to do
Open up the door and I'll be walking through
You know I want to serve you,
You know I always want to do my part.
I don't know how to do it, I don't know where to start
I'm reaching here inside me and I hope I'm gonna get it
From the heart, from the heart,
From the heart.

I've got this burden, I've been dragging it around
It gets so heavy that it weighs my spirit down
I've got to open up my fists, loosen up my grip and let it go
Let it go.
I don't know how to do it, I don't know where to start
I'm reaching here inside me and
I hope I'm gonna get it
From the heart, from the heart,
From the heart.

—Sam Beasley

———————————— PRAYER ————————————

Inspiring

My Creator, to inspire is to breathe in, to inhale air into my lungs. To inspire is to encourage to enthusiasm—literally to cause myself or others *to have the heart to be with you*. To inspire is to arouse a feeling that leads to creativity.

I'm worth taking the time to find things that inspire me. I'm worth finding materials to read and listen to before I go out into the world, before I get into action. I'm worth taking the time to remember that I have a connection to you, my Source, that I'm not alone, that I'm being guided. I'm worth finding my own daily inspiration, to write it down and carry it with me. I'm worth getting inspired through prayer and meditation, to listen to that guidance.

When I'm inspired, I'm inspiring, and both feel great! When I'm inspiring, I'm a man of attraction and I like being of service. I really appreciate inspiration from others—my friends, my partner, and unknown messengers I meet.

When I'm inspired, I produce, and I love what I produce from inspiration—it's exciting and I'm filled with passion in the process. When I'm inspired, I come alive. I feel inspiration coursing through me. I feel *enthusiasm*—I feel my connection to All That Is.

I'm worth inspiring—it inspires me to worth!

Thank you, God!

CHAPTER 17

OUR RELATIONSHIPS WITH ANIMALS, PLANTS, AND THE NATURAL WORLD ARE PRAYERS

One touch of nature makes the whole world kin.

—William Shakespeare, English playwright

Forest Cathedral

When I was a kid, our family lived in southern Germany for several years, where my dad was stationed at a military base. The housing area on base was surrounded by a forest—a beautiful Bavarian forest of tall trees very close together, so that there were almost no branches down below, but a thick canopy at the very top. The forest was a very spiritual place—mystical, even magical. I often walked in the woods early in the morning before school and was always filled with a sense of the numinous, the holy, the divine. To me, it was God's cathedral and I could feel His presence all around me.

Now Germany has many magnificent man-made cathedrals, for sure. Built from stones or bricks, illuminated by stunning stained-glass windows, furnished with centuries-old hand-hewn wooden pews, infused with the scent of incense and beeswax candles. Deeply spiritual places, to be sure.

But to my mind—the mind of a child—no place was as holy as the forest. The soft carpet of evergreen needles underfoot, the beautiful green canopy overhead, supported by pillars of strong straight tree trunks. Blueberries grew in patches on the floor of the forest—eating them was my way of taking communion—ingesting a bit of God's creation, taking it into my body, becoming One with God.

In the decades since leaving Germany, I've traveled to many countries around the world and visited numerous holy sites and spiritual places. But the forest is still my favorite, for God created it with His own hands, His own breath, His own imagination and creativity. The forest is simple, pure, and the best church I could ever spend time in. The forest feeds my soul in ways that man-made buildings never can.

The forest is my prayer—then, now, and always.

> The clearest way into the Universe is through a forest wilderness.
>
> **—John Muir, pioneering environmentalist**

> I understood at a very early age that in nature,
> I felt everything I should feel in church but never did.
> Walking in the woods,
> I felt in touch with the universe and with the spirit of the universe.
>
> **—Alice Walker, author**

The World According to Connor

The first gift my grandson Connor gave me was a handful of gravel. He didn't just bend down, scoop it up, and hand it to me. He had to come and find me. When he spotted me, he came running up to me and reached out his fist and dumped his little gift of wet gravel into my hand, then he wanted me to show it to him. He was extraordinarily fascinated with it and pleased. He was one year old and giving me something incredible.

I didn't realize it, but he was seeing something I *couldn't* see. I made the mistake of thinking there was nothing there other than what I could see—a normal dirty little pile of average wet gravel. I didn't realize for quite some time that there was *something* there. I'm truly sorry to say that, when he wasn't looking, I dropped it on the ground. I would love to still have that little pile of gravel.

All my grandkids did this: they wanted to share that *something* they could see—in dandelions, sparrows, spiders, worms, cats, or grass. Whatever it was, it was extraordinary, and it absolutely caught their eye and imagination. And I don't know what it was. And here is what sticks with me: I think they were right. There really was *something* there. And I can't see it.

It isn't that I don't ever see it—get me near water and it's the only thing I can see—that *something*. I can't tell you what it is, but I can tell you that it's there and I can't take my eyes off it. Whenever I am near a river or at the beach, I absolutely hate to leave because of it. When my inner adult makes me leave, I can't wait to get back. Whatever it is, it fills me with the joy and wonder that had engulfed Connor five years ago when he held out his tiny hand and gave me the gravel.

Here is my guess: we all could see it once and mostly we can't now. I still see it in water and I'm so grateful for that. I hope you still see it somewhere. I think it has to do with what we sense is true, but we can't prove. I think it might have something to do with why we pray.

I keep everything that Connor and my other grandkids give me now. I believe them. Maybe, when I'm older, I will look at it and see what they saw when they were younger. Hope so.

I pray to someday see the world through the eyes of a child.

> No, we don't need more sleep. It's our souls that are tired, not our bodies, We need nature. We need magic. We need adventure. We need freedom. We need truth. We need stillness. We don't need more sleep, we need to wake up and live.
>
> —Brooke Hampton, writer

> Water isn't just for drinking or washing.
> Water has its own spirit. Water is alive.
> Water has memory.
> Water knows how you treat it, water knows you.
> You should get to know water, too.
>
> —Wabinoquay Otsoquaykwhan, Anishinaabe Nation

What is WISDOM?

Wondrous
Insight
Seeing
Deeply
Offering
Miracles

_____ PRAYER _____

I am the origin of all things.
In me the whole universe originates and dissolves.
All this is strung in me, as a row of jewels on
a thread.
I am the wetness of water
the radiance in the moon and the sun
I am the sweet fragrance in earth, and the brilliance
in fire
I Am the life in all beings.
—The Bhagavad Gita

_____ PRAYER _____

May all beings everywhere awaken to
the inherent goodness that dwells
within themselves
and all others.
—Anonymous

PRAYER

River of Peace

I am called to walk by water.

My heart jumps at the sight of any river

And sound of waves pulls me to the shore.

All thoughts disappear

And my eyes can only scan

the surface and the depths.

I long to see fish and otters

And I am at peace.

I can't say why it's true

I can only say

Thank You.

PRAYER

May I be safe and protected.

May I be healthy and strong.

May I be truly happy.

May all beings far and near,

all beings young and old,

beings in every direction,

be held in great loving-kindness.

> May they be safe and protected.
>
> May they be healthy and strong.
>
> May they be truly happy.
>
> **—Jack Kornfield, Buddhist author**

CHAPTER 18

PAIN, SUFFERING, LOSS, AND DEATH ARE PRAYERS

The terrible gift of a terrible illness is that is has in fact taught me to live in the moment. But when I look at these mementos, I realize that I am learning more than to seize the day. In losing my future, the mundane begins to sparkle. The things I love—the things I should love—become clearer, brighter. This is transcendence, the past and the future experienced together in moments where I can see a flicker of eternity.

—Kate Bowler, cancer patient, author of *Everything Happens for a Reason: And Other Lies I've Loved*

Kathryn, Cancer, and God

I called my friend Sam to complain about the injustice: "I just got word that my friend Kathryn has been diagnosed with stage four pancreatic cancer. She's only sixty-eight years old. She's been sober for thirty years; she hasn't had a cigarette in twenty-nine years; and she hasn't eaten sugar for twenty-eight years. She flosses after every meal and her teeth are perfect. She's trim and athletic. She and her husband go biking very weekend. Their summer vacations are biking across Europe with friends. She's done everything right and still...*still* she gets cancer!"

"So, let me ask you a question," Sam said. "Are you her Higher Power? Are *you* her God?"

"Well, no."

"But what you're telling me is that you want to overrule her Higher Power," Sam said. "You think YOU know what's right for Kathryn."

"Uh..."

"For all we know, this might just be the best year of her life," Sam said.

"Oh. I hadn't thought of it like that."

"Most people don't," Sam continued. "In fact, your friend Kathryn probably isn't thinking about it like that either. But the truth is, we don't know that the cancer might not come bearing gifts...and this last year of her life might be incredibly good."

Could Sam be right? Kathryn had expressed many worries, concerns, and complaints over the ten years that I knew her. Chief among them was the absence of an exit strategy from the high-stress business she owned. She often complained that her husband John was not sufficiently sensitive to her emotional needs. She said she felt lonely much of the time and had no close friends. And she fretted about her two daughters: Chloe was overweight and Dianne wasn't interested in getting married. Kathryn lamented the lack of grandchildren. Clearly, hers wasn't the picture-perfect family Kathryn thought it ought to be.

Underlying her concerns and complaints was a chronic refrain of fear and mistrust. Kathryn said she had a hard time trusting people. Myriad fears haunted her daily life: fear that her business wasn't making enough money, fear that she'd miss a deadline or make a mistake; fear of what others thought of her; fear of abandonment; fears for her daughters' happiness...her fears seemed endless.

To any outside observer, these worries seemed baseless and irrational. Kathryn was a wealthy woman with a long marriage to a handsome, successful man; she had two lovely homes; she leased a new Mercedes every three years; her daughters were talented, attractive, and smart; and her family enjoyed a lifestyle anyone would envy. But the fears were still there—they had nothing to do with objective conditions.

Within a week of her diagnosis, all that began to change. Kathryn's husband took a leave of absence from his job and devoted himself to caring for her. He moved her business out of their home and put it up for sale while she was in hospital, so when she came home all she had to do was focus on her health.

When I went to visit her in the hospital, I expected to find her crying and fearful—her usual response to anything bad. But the Kathryn who greeted me from her hospital bed was relaxed and glowing. Her room was filled with flowers, cards, and balloons. Her entire family was gathered there with her—her husband John, daughters Chloe and Dianne, her sister Suzanne and Suzanne's fiancé. Kathryn was basking in their love and attention. She told me that she felt peaceful and serene, trusting God that all would be well.

For the next seven months, Kathryn's life looked like the solar system—with Kathryn as the sun—family and friends orbiting around her. She received calls and visitors daily. John doted on her. Chloe was at the house every day and Kathryn's sister Suzanne came frequently, too. Dianne got married and Kathryn rallied to participate in the wedding. The happy couple got pregnant, fulfilling one of Kathryn's fondest wishes—for a grandchild. With her business gone, Kathryn had the time and money to do anything she wanted—with her devoted husband by her side. They went on outings to the local arboretum and gardens, museums, movies, and their weekend home up the coast.

I think back on what my friend Sam had told me: "This might very well be the best year of Kathryn's life." From all appearances, it was. Her cares and concerns of previous years simply disappeared— along with the fear that had gripped her. Her final months were filled with love, laughter, lively conversations, companionship, holidays and special occasions with her family, and treasured moments with loving friends. Kathryn got everything she'd ever wanted. Her prayers had been answered.

As is often the way with us humans, Kathryn finally realized that much of what she thought was missing had actually been there all along. In the words of French writer Colette: "What a wonderful life I've had! I only wish I'd realized it sooner."

Cancer had come into Kathryn's life—bearing gifts.

> Buddha said that fortune changes like the swish of a horse's tail.
> Tomorrow could be the first day of thirty years of quadriplegia...
> The more you open to life, the less death becomes the enemy.
> When you start using death as a means of focusing on life,
> then everything becomes just as it is, just this moment,
> an extraordinary opportunity to be really alive.
> **—Stephen Levine, poet, spiritual teacher, author of *Who Dies?***

> Darkness deserves gratitude. It is the alleluia point
> at which we learn to understand that all growth
> does not take place in the sunlight.
>
> **—Joan D. Chittister, Benedictine nun,
>   theologian, author**

Every Wrong Turn Turns Around

I've been on the planet for over six decades. By anyone's standards, I have experienced losses during my life. I met every loss with fear, anger, resentment, regret, hopelessness, or some combination of those emotions. These haven't been my proudest moments.

I've lost two wives, a career I loved, a wonderful business, my spine was injured, my left arm was paralyzed. I was briefly houseless. I lost my entire community. I never thought I'd have children or grandchildren. I thought I had destroyed my relationships with my sisters and my extended family. At times I lost my pride, my sense of masculinity, my esteem.

These were painful experiences that, at the time of each occurrence, I believed would cause permanent loss in my life. Did I have a glimmer of faith? Nope. Just my absolute certainty that my life was ruined, that I'd die a pauper, that I would live without meaningful work or love, I would be crippled, I'd never play guitar again, and I'd spend the rest of my life alone and lonely. I must have been really fun to be around.

Was my assessment of gloom accurate? Not. One. Bit. Not even a smidgen of right. Here is what really happened:

- For almost thirty years I've been happily married with the love of my life
- I have work that I love
- I own successful businesses
- My spine healed
- My left arm works again
- I joyfully play guitar
- I live in a wonderful home
- I enjoy a community filled with loving, fun friends
- I have three wonderful children and I'm "Papa" to two sweet grandkids
- I love my sisters and cousins and I love being with them
- My retirement is safe

In my assessment that all was lost, I was as mistaken as I could be.

Doom was my go-to belief every time I experienced loss, and then a ray of light appeared through a crack in that belief system. Many years ago, in the midst of a doom moment, I had the thought that I had never allowed myself to check and see if I had been accurate all those years. I got the brilliant idea to create an exercise sheet with three columns:

What happened?	How did I think it would turn out?	How did it really turn out?

As I did the exercise, I discovered that the second column, "How did I think it would turn out?" was entirely inaccurate. Fortunately for me, my ability to assess tragic outcomes was absolutely flawed. Every wrong turn turned around and led to an incredible life!

I'm grateful to say that my old prayer, "I'm doomed," has evolved into something a little more honest and useful: "Every wrong turn turns around. This seeming loss will turn around as well."

My favorite version of this prayer is the anthem chorus to the Chumbawamba song "Tubthumping":

> **"I get knocked down, but I get up again**
> **You're never gonna keep me down!"**

Once I get that earworm in my mind and have sung it non-stop for a couple of hours, you're never gonna keep me down! Sing it with me!

"I get knocked down, but I get up again..."

Someone I loved once gave me a box full of darkness.
It took me years to understand that this, too, was a gift.

—Mary Oliver, poet

Barn's burnt down…
Now I can see the moon.

**—Mizuta Masahide, seventeenth-century
Japanese samurai**

As You Grieve...

ACCEPT that grief is the price we pay for loving.

BE GENTLE and patient with yourself.

CONFIDE in people you trust.

DON'T JUDGE your feelings as good or bad—just feel them.

EXPECT the unexpected—you may say or do surprising things.

FEEL your pain and know that it will pass.

GET THROUGH each day, each moment, as best you can.

HUG those you love...friends, family, and pets.

INVITE your grief to teach you lessons of love and life.

JUST BE with your sadness.

KNOW that others may feel awkward in the face of your grief.

LISTEN and respond to your body and its needs.

MAKE NO big decisions while you're grieving.

NEVER LET others deny your right to your feelings.

OPEN your heart and mind to this experience—
  don't fight it.

PEER into the mysteries of life and death.

QUESTION the meaning of your life and find
  new answers.

REST and sleep—it's good for healing.

SPEND lots of time with those who love and comfort you.

TAKE YOUR TIME—grief has its own timetable.

UNDERSTAND that others may do or say unhelpful
  things in their attempts to help.

VEER away from people who try to tell you when or how
  to grieve.

WITNESS the importance of grieving for others, too.

X-PRESS your feelings in ways that help you—talking,
  writing, crying, painting, singing, etc.

YEARN to know the reason "why" even though there may
  be no answer.

ZERO IN on what makes living worthwhile.

...TAKE GOOD CARE OF YOURSELF.

—BJ Gallagher

————————— PRAYER —————————

In the Fall

In the fall, when my limbs are stripped bare

By a cold unwanted wind,

Every memory of cycles is gone from me.

Bare now is bare forever.

I remember fruit and leaves

And sun and breezes.

I can almost smile.

Almost.

Bare now is bare forever.

Divine, when all is lost, grant me grace to

remember Spring.

————————— PRAYER —————————

I Trust That What I've Left Behind Has Led Me Ever Forward.

Dearest God, many times, I've heard my voice pleading "Please, please, please, bring (it, her, me) back and let me start again." When I focused on the void of what was gone, I felt the pain of the loss. The memory of what was and the void of the now were all that existed. Of those two, what used to be seemed a lot more appealing than the void.

I forget that all voids are filled. Sometimes quickly, sometimes slowly, every void is filled. Always.

God, if we know in advance what we want next, and we get it, we hardly notice that we had to create a void so that we'd have someplace to put the new fulfillment. However, in those moments when we are unaware that a shift is occurring, and unaware that we are awaiting the new, that void only looks like loss.

In those moments, it's easy and comforting to look back and romanticize the past: "But, it was sooooo good! It/he/she/I was perfect, no matter what I said!" It really takes some work to recognize that this is one of those times when the void is just a signpost of something that lies ahead.

If, on some Christmas Eve, a husband looks out the window and sees his car is missing, he might really panic. If he gets up the next morning and his wife has a shiny new car for him sitting in the driveway, he will understand why his car had to be missing. If, two years later, he looks out the window on Christmas Eve and his car is missing, he might only be excited. How seldom we recognize the void in that way.

I know I have voids ahead of me. Maybe one of these times I will see the void and be excited and curious about what lies ahead. Today, my prayer is:

**I trust that what I've left behind
has led me ever forward.**

———————— PRAYER ————————

I Am a Vessel

I am a vessel here to be filled
Empty and ready and seeking God's will.
I have my wants and they're wanting me still,
Still, I swear I'm a vessel and I'm here to be filled.

I have been dreaming of all I have lost.
Hard to believe life might hold such a cost.
There's hope in the Spirit,
In our heavenly friend,
Who's sure to bring comfort
That these long tears might end.

I've been a fighter, fighting to win
Losing each battle, to fight them again.
My hope is surrender, my chance—to give in
And learn to live gently and seek peace again

I yearn for a pure heart while laden with fear,
Often forgetting that mercy is here.
I long for the right road, I'm seeking it still
My hunger will pass, and my thirst will be filled.

I am a vessel here to be filled

Empty and ready and seeking God's will.

I have my wants and they're haunting me still,

Still, I swear I'm a vessel and I'm here to be filled.

—Sam Beasley

CHAPTER 19

GRATITUDE IS YOUR PRAYER

Gratitude unlocks the fullness of life.
It turns what we have into enough, and more.
It turns denial into acceptance, chaos to order, confusion to clarity.
It can turn a meal into a feast, a house into a home, a stranger into a friend. Gratitude makes sense of our past, brings peace for today,
and creates a vision for tomorrow.

—Melody Beattie, therapist, author

Gratitude Dispels Financial Fear

My friend Tom Feltenstein often asks, "Have you ever noticed how life seems to keep giving you more of what you *don't* want?" He asks this in order to make an important point.

One of the primary reasons we keep getting more of what we don't want is the way we think—how our minds work. The mind is a mismatch detector—it always notices what's wrong before it notices what's right. Consider a couple of examples:

You walk into an art gallery and there are ten paintings hanging on the wall. Nine of them are straight and one is a little crooked. Where does your eye go? To the crooked painting—instantly. Your attention will be grabbed by what's wrong with the situation, not what's right with it.

A personal example: I had a tooth pulled not too long ago, and I noticed that for many weeks after the tooth extraction, my tongue kept going to the gap between my molars where my tooth had been. It happened again and again, throughout the day. My tongue was "worrying" over the missing molar. Did my tongue pay any attention to the other twenty-nine teeth that are fine? No. It just kept going back to the empty space.

I *know* that my mind is a mismatch detector—I teach this in my seminars. And yet, I could hardly stop myself from focusing on what was wrong in my mouth, rather than what was right. Knowing that what my tongue was doing didn't seem to stop me from doing it. Sometimes self-knowledge is the booby prize—if it doesn't help us change our behavior.

My wife and I wrote a book titled *Wealth and Well-Being*, in which we outline a good antidote for "what's missing thinking." We calls it "scheduled gratitude." Here's how I explained it to my friend Michael recently:

I asked: "Do you like where you live?"

Michael's answer: "I love where I live!"

"Good. Then here's what you do. Every morning and every evening, for ten minutes or so, walk through your home and notice the things that you really love. An old quilt your mother made, a vase you inherited from your great-aunt, a piece of furniture you treasure, a room you love to spend time in, a piece of art, or whatever it is that you love. Touch these things, run your fingers over them, and say out loud, 'I love this; I'd like more of this.' This is an act of 'active appreciation' in which you tell the Universe that you are deeply grateful for these blessings. You show appreciation and you ask for more. The Universe is a giant YES machine—it will always send you more of what you pay attention to."

I summarized: "If you don't like what you're getting in your life, change your prayer. How you live your life is a form of prayer; what you pay attention to is a form of prayer; what you express gratitude for is a form of prayer. If you want your life to be different, your prayer must be different."

I added: "Schedule this time on your calendar, just as you would any appointment. Because if you don't schedule it, you'll start forgetting to do it. This is scheduled gratitude—active appreciation. I do it every day myself—three times a day—at 9 a.m., 1 p.m., and 6 p.m. Makes all the difference in my day!"

Michael has followed my instructions for some time now, and it has made an enormous difference. He told me: "I feel like a very rich person. I walk around happy almost all the time. I notice what's right in my home, in my business, and in my life. I give gratitude for my pets as I stroke their fur. I am grateful for the wonderful business I have built and count my blessings when I go to my office every day. I give thanks and appreciation for my wonderful family, my loving friends, my car, my garden, my fruit trees...and, of course, money in the bank. I say a quiet prayer of gratitude every time a check arrives. And I write 'thank you' on every check I write, grateful that I have money to pay my bills."

Michael now understands that gratitude is more than attitude—it's action. And nothing transforms fear like gratitude in action.

If the only prayer you ever say in your entire life is "thank you," it will be enough.

—Meister Eckhart, German priest and mystic

Appreciating What I Love and Appreciating Life Itself Feels Good... *And* I Get More of What I Appreciate.

Imagine if yesterday you spent one minute appreciating something in your life. Now imagine if throughout today you spent one minute, and another minute, and another minute, and by the end of the day it totaled *one hour* appreciating different aspects of life. Moments of appreciating are blossoms on wonderful fruit trees in life. One blossom produces one juicy cherry. Put more blossoms on your trees and the next thing you know you'll have the best cherry pie you've ever tasted!

It seems we learn to appreciate in the smallest and simplest of ways, and the learning keeps building. Take a moment to slowly take a deep breath, fill your lungs, relaxing your brow, softening your shoulders. Let it out slowly while you notice your thinking and vision seemed to clear a little. Isn't that wonderful? That's appreciation and that was easy!

Look around you. Do you see some object you love? Isn't it wonderful to have this object in your life? (I really love coffee and guitars, so my coffee maker and my instruments are my favorite possessions!)

Look around you. Do you see beauty? Don't you love a beautiful landscape, a beautiful face, a stunning sunrise? That is appreciation! That is worth doing! Do it as often as you want. You'll be amazed at how good you feel. You will be amazed that what you appreciate seems to show up more often than before!

> Let us rise up and be thankful,
> for if we didn't learn a lot today, at least we learned a little;
> and if we didn't learn a little, at least we didn't get sick;
> and if we got sick, at least we didn't die;
> so, let us all be thankful.
>
> **—The Buddha**

We Give Thanks By...

AWAKENING each day with an attitude of gratitude.

BEING HUMBLE about our role in the universe.

COUNTING OUR BLESSINGS...often.

DELIGHTING in simple pleasures.

ENCOURAGING those who need our support.

FORGIVING those who have disappointed or hurt us.

GIVING what we can to help others.

HUGGING our loved ones—family, friends, and pets.

INCLUDING those who have no close friends or family.

JUGGLING our commitments to both work and family.

KEEPING A LIGHT IN THE WINDOW for those who
    have lost their way.

LOVING others unconditionally.

MAKING ROOM for one more person at the table.

NEVER FORGETTING to offer a prayer of thanks.

OPENING our hearts and our wallets to those in need.

PREPARING warm, nourishing holiday meals.

QUIETING our minds with prayer and meditation.

RECOGNIZING that blessings can show up in
surprising ways.

SPEAKING kindly and compassionately to others.

TAPPING INTO SPIRITUAL WISDOM to guide us.

UNDERSTANDING that blessings are meant to
be shared.

VEERING AWAY from resentments and anger.

WORKING for an end to hunger, both physical
and spiritual.

X-PRESSING appreciation for all that others do for us.

YEARNING FOR AND WORKING FOR PEACE.

ZEROING IN on what's truly important in life.

—BJ Gallagher

———————————— PRAYER ————————————

Joy! Joy! Joy!

Joy feels so *good*, I choose joy. I choose to think those thoughts I know bring out joy in me. I choose to find new ways of thinking to experience joy. I choose to experience joy in bringing joy to others.

Every day, wonderful things happen. Some are big, some are small and they all bring joy. Today I watched a stunning sunrise on a valley I've never seen. I had a simple, pleasant conversation with a young woman who had a lovely accent and a beautiful smile. I spoke with a young soldier who told me she was living out of *the best choice she had ever made in her life!* (How often do we get to hear someone say that?)

I find joy in appreciation, joy in fascination, joy in the kindness of others, joy in laughter, joy in smiling, joy in listing my blessings. I am taking off my "joy blinders" and I find joy all around me. I can't help but sing!

———————————— PRAYER ————————————

Thank God I've Changed My Focus!

All That Is, I can't remember the last time something "bad" happened to me. I'm grateful for this change of focus!

I remember going through life with my teeth clenched, already angry at what was certain to go wrong. I was waiting for the next bad thing to happen. I remember hopeless defeat. "Nothing ever goes right."

I remember not knowing I was creating this life with my Source. I'm so thankful to know that now. I'm thankful to know that my interpreting some experience as "bad" doesn't make it bad—it just makes it *feel* bad. With the smallest amount of gratitude—even when I don't know why I should be grateful—these "bad things" transform.

Thank you for the slow drivers ahead of me who are helping me slow down. Thank you for the tax bill helping me keep my agreement to not debt. Thank you for the contract that ends and creates space for a bigger contract. Thank you for the barking dog that inspired me to move to these quiet, beautiful mountains. Thank you, thank you, thank you!

PRAYER

My Gratitude Blesses My Life. I Am Surrounded With Care.

I find peace in my financial stability. I am most aware of prosperity when I'm grateful for it. I am most grateful for my prosperity when I identify the ways it shows up in my life. I have enough.

God, there have been times in my life when I lived in deprivation and the constant threat of not enough, of self-disregard. The incredible lack of care took a toll on my mental and emotional state and serenity was not a word I knew. As I surrendered to self-care, I began to understand that fiscal stability can play an essential part. It's one of many pieces of accepting blessings.

Every blessing can disappear in the moment I lose gratitude. It's as if everything in an abundant bank account of self-care suddenly vanishes. I can re-fund that account in the moment I find gratitude in any single piece of this glorious life. In gratitude I am surrounded with care. It is my greatest tool and my greatest wealth.

Thank you, God.

—————————— PRAYER ——————————

I'm Stretching Out My Limits. Thank You for This Freedom!

I'm done with disregard for my visions, wants, dreams! I've given a restricted life a good try and I'm done! Today I'm stretching out my limits. A bell is going off when I think the words "can't" and "won't." A light starts flashing when I use restricting phrases about any aspect of me and my life.

I'm grateful that I'm changing the truth! I'm letting go of my need to be right about these limitations. I'm willing to acknowledge "I have been saying this restricting thought is the truth, but it isn't absolutely so."

Yes, I *can* afford to fly first-class. Yes, I can have exactly what I want. My income is not maxed out and I'm inspired to see it grow. My business has not reached a stalemate—it's experiencing a fresh beginning. There is no "maximum delay allowance" in any area of my life. *There is enough money!*

There is enough time for me to do what I love! Thank you Thank you Thank you!

Today I'm the biggest cheerleader of my life. I'm encouraging, hopeful, positive, heartening, inspiring, reassuring, promising, boosting, uplifting. I'm eager to see my old limiting "truths" fall away. I'm excited about the boundless unknown blessings coming my way.

My prayer: Today I am stretching out my limits!

CHAPTER 20

GENEROSITY AND GIVING ARE PRAYERS

Keep yourself like an empty vessel for God to fill. Keep pouring out yourself to help others so that God can keep filling you up with His spirit. The more you give, the more you will have for yourself. God will see that you are kept filled as long as you are giving to others. But if you selfishly try to keep all for yourself, you are soon blocked off from God, your source of supply, and you will become stagnant. To be clear, a lake must have an inflow and an outflow.

—Richmond Walker, *Twenty-Four Hours a Day*

My Greatest Lessons

In 2001, I did a series of interviews with millionaires about the process of going from poverty to wealth. I had twenty-eight questions I asked each of them. The very last question was, "Is there anything I should have asked you, but I didn't know to ask it?" Every one of them had more than one answer, and every answer was about prayer, gratitude, and giving.

These happy, grateful wealthy people shared thoughts with me that were, at some level, new to me. I had previously heard the essence of their thoughts and experience. When I heard it again from them, I understood it in a very new way.

They each shared about the power of prayer in their life. In poverty, they each reached a moment when they were told to embrace prayer and they each chose to embrace it. From their descriptions, they weren't just embracing prayer, they had it wrapped in a bear hug and were keeping it close every day. They began their days in prayer, and three of them began each day in prayer with others. They spoke so powerfully about prayer that I realized I was being given a lesson that I could not decline to learn and embrace for my own. I did. I began to pray and to write prayers and I've never stopped writing prayers. Some of those prayers are included in this book.

The other thing they each talked about was giving. These people were extraordinarily generous givers—the most generous people I had ever met. They spoke to me about giving in a way that I have never forgotten. I again realized I was being let in on a "secret" and that I needed to set aside my objective interviewer hat and accept and adopt the lessons.

Lesson #1: Pray. Pray as a way of reminding ourselves that we are not alone in this life. Pray as a way of reminding ourselves that it is okay to tell the truth about what we want, that maybe, if we get it, we will use what we want in the service of others. Pray as a reminder that we are not It, that claiming to be It may not be the best approach. Pray as a way to quiet inner turmoil and have a little peace—that life is so much easier and we are so much more creative when we have inner peace.

Lesson #2: Give. Give willingly. Give in joy. Give to what matters to you. Be ready to give. Give when it's requested. That last part really surprised me: *Give when it's requested*. In the years that have passed, I've learned so much about this. At first, I tried giving whether or not it was requested and learned that it doesn't always work out so well. Now I am ready to give to what matters to me and I give when it's requested. I've had a very recent experience being with many people who had just lost *everything* in a massive disaster. In the first week following the disaster, I offered money. All but one of them turned it down. I had to wait until the others were ready to request help. I have such respect for them for not accepting it before they were ready!

Lesson #3: Give up "I can do this by myself." If someone has a life you want, and they offer to show you how they did it, as quickly as you can, say, "Yes! Please show me!" Then listen closely and do exactly what they did. If it worked for them, it will probably work for you. Each one of these interviewees did exactly that. And if you know someone who has a life you want, and they don't offer to help you, ask them to tell you how they did it. Most successful people are so proud of what they've accomplished, they just wish someone would ask them how they did it.

The things that I learned in these interviews were the greatest lessons I've ever had, and they completely transformed my life. If there is only one thing that I can be grateful for in this life, it's this: that Something told me "Kid, you better listen and take advantage of what these people are telling you," and that I found the willingness to do that.

Of the things I learned from these people, one line has always stayed with me. I heard it, adopted it, I've used it since, and I can confirm that it's true:

"I wish someone had told me sooner about this giving thing. You know, you can't out-give God."

> We make a living by what we get.
> We make a life by what we give.
> **—Winston Churchill, British statesman**

Giving Back to the Universe

A few years ago I was having a hard time financially. It had been a slow year for business; I'd had some big medical bills; and I had not been as careful with my money as I should have been. It was

November, and I didn't know how I was going to make it through the end of the year. I called my friend Anna to ask her advice. She had a good head for money.

I tearfully explained my predicament. She listened quietly. She was kind and sympathetic, completely understanding. She did not judge or scold. "You want my advice?" she asked, when I had finished telling her my sad story.

"Well, sure," I replied, "that's why I called you."

"Tithe," she said simply.

I couldn't believe my ears. "You don't understand," I objected. "I just told you—I don't have any money coming in, I've got all these bills piled up, and I don't know how I'm going to meet the mortgage next month. I can't tithe—I have nothing to tithe with!"

"Well, you asked my advice, and I'm giving it to you," she said matter-of-factly. "All I have to share with you is my own experience. If you start to tithe, you shift your relationship with God. It is an act of faith in which you essentially say, 'I know I will be taken care of, so I can give this money back to God.' It works for me and it works for lots of other people I know, too."

I knew in my heart of hearts that Anna was right. Tithing was something I had wanted to do for a long time, but I was afraid—afraid I would not have enough money to meet my needs, afraid to give away 10 percent of my income, afraid of financial insecurity. I had heard other people talk about tithing in the past, and being a spiritual person, I liked the idea—but my fear always got the better of me.

"Here's what I'd suggest," Anna continued, "Why don't you call Naomi and ask her what her experience has been with tithing. Call Constance too, and see what she has to say. Then decide if it's right for you."

I thanked Anna for her advice, and immediately dialed Naomi's number. She was more than happy to tell me about her experience with tithing. She had been in similar financial straits a few years earlier, and Anna had given her the same advice she'd given me. Reluctantly, Naomi agreed to do it. She started by tithing to a twelve-step community of which she was a member, because Anna had instructed her to "give to the spiritual community that nurtures you." Naomi took a check to the office of this twelve-step program every time she got paid (she was self-employed in the real estate business). "The first time I tithed," Naomi told me, "I sold a $400,000 house the very next week! I made a great commission. I'm sure it was a direct result of my tithing."

After a while, Anna suggested that Naomi start tithing to her local synagogue, since she had been born and raised Jewish. "I'm not going to do that," Naomi protested. "I lost my faith years ago, and I'm not going to give them any money." Anna nudged Naomi: "Just try it. Do it a few times. See what happens." So the next time Naomi got paid, she drove to the synagogue and gave them a check. Before long, the rabbi invited her to come to a special event at the synagogue. She went. She met a few people she liked, and she started going to more events. Her heart began softening toward the Jewish faith she had rejected, and over time she gradually felt more and more a part of this community. Finally, Naomi became an official member of the temple.

About this time, her young nephew turned thirteen and it was time for him to have his bar mitzvah. She knew that her sister didn't have much money, so Naomi offered to pay for the bar mitzvah. Naomi had been estranged from her sister, but she loved her nephew very much, and she wanted to do this for him. Over the months of planning the ceremony and the party, Naomi and her sister gradually worked through their differences and were reconciled. The bar mitzvah was a wonderful day for the whole family.

In short, Naomi's commitment to tithe 10 percent of whatever she earned transformed her life. Tithing did more than put her on sound financial ground, it brought her back to her Jewish faith, it strengthened the bond between her and her nephew, and it reunited her with her sister. She was living a life of miracles.

If I had any doubt about the efficacy of tithing, it disappeared in listening to Naomi's story. Tithing means acknowledging that no matter how little one has, there are always other people who are worse off. Tithing means saying to God, "I trust that You will provide for me, and I am willing to give back 10 percent to do Your work in the world." Tithing lifts the burden of fear from my heart, and replaces it with trust. Tithing to a spiritual organization that gives me spiritual sustenance is the best way of saying "thanks" for all that I have received.

I once heard Jack Canfield (coauthor of *Chicken Soup for the Soul*) talk about tithing and its role in his life. He said, "Both my coauthor and I have been tithing for many years and we think it's an important part of our business success. (Their *Chicken Soup* books have sold over 60 million copies!) But I have to tell you, it was a lot easier to write those checks in the early years, when they were smaller. It's kind of hard to sit down today and write tithing checks for $100,000!" I laughed when he said that. The truth is, that's a problem I'd *love* to have!

I've been tithing for several years now, ever since the phone conversations I had with Anna and Naomi. I don't sell real estate, and I haven't had the success of *Chicken Soup*, but my finances have stabilized and the peace of mind I feel is wonderful. Tithing shifted my relationship to God from one of "fearful child asking God's protection" to "adult partner with God" in doing good in the world. It feels wonderful.

Giving opens the way for receiving.

—Florence Scovel Shinn, author

If you want something, give it.

—Deepak Chopra, Indian-born American author

How to Lend a HELPING HAND...

Hearing what's needed

Eager to contribute

Listening with compassion

Paying attention to the little things

Intuitively understanding what's helpful and what's not

Never overstepping your bounds

Going out of your way for a true friend

Healing love, healing touch

Asking "What can I do to help?"

Never assuming that you know what's best

Desiring to serve and contribute to others' wellbeing

—— PRAYER ——

Let Me Be In Service Today—It Fills Me with Blessings!

Dearest God, whenever I have the opportunity to serve, every blessing I've ever received wraps around me like a favorite old jacket. Each moment of transformation, every wonderful hug, each glorious piece of music I've written, sung, or heard comes rushing back and swirls around me. Joy is in my every breath.

God, let me be in service today. I've received so much and have so much to give. I can give it all freely and never give up anything. Each act of service increases my experience of wealth infinitely. Each act of service increases my love and appreciation for this stunning life.

Let me be in service today. I am called to reach out and give. I am filled with gratitude.

—— PRAYER ——

To Whom Much Is Given, from Him Much Is Expected

When I first heard the term "noblesse oblige" back in college, I knew it applied to me. God, you have given me so much—intelligence, creativity, imagination, several talents and skills—that I understand I am required to do something with all those blessings. They are not just for my benefit—they are to be used to help others. I am obliged to be a good steward of my gifts—to use them wisely and not squander them in selfish activities.

Thank you, God, for the gifts of social capital: my parents who raised me and taught me the value of honesty and hard work, my son who loves me and challenges me to be the best parent I can be, and my friends who provide an invaluable support network. Some people are born with financial capital—you gave me the gifts of social capital. Either type of capital is a great treasure and both are to be used wisely. Thank you for my social capital—my family and friends.

I ask that you guide me and show me how best to fulfill your expectations of me, and the expectations I have for myself. Please show me how to give back what has so generously been given to me.

My prayer: To whom much is given, from him much is expected. God, what do you expect from me today?

———————————— PRAYER ————————————

I Am Blessed with Abundance and I Give with Joy and I'm Filled with Appreciation!

Higher Power...I have an envelope labeled "Giving" and I love to put money in it. When I'm called to give, I love taking the money out and giving it freely. I don't miss one dollar of the money that I've given. I know only continued abundance.

I have a value, Service, and I love giving service even more. I have never missed one hour of the time I've given. I've been so blessed in these experiences of service. I'm ready now to serve. No matter how much time I spend in service, more time arrives in my life.

I don't know which comes first: giving or receiving. I only know they are always possible and always a gift. Always.

Higher Power, bring me the opportunity to give and I will give. Bring me the opportunity to serve and I will serve. I have no fear of having too little.

I'm filled with appreciation!

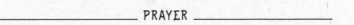

——————————— PRAYER ———————————

Please Remind Me I'm a Lily of the Field

I pray I never forget that everything I have ever had or ever will have was already here when I arrived. It will be here when I'm gone. While I'm here it all gets moved around a little, but it's all still here.

I pray I never grasp too tightly. Give me the job of moving it around, a little to this person, a little to that person. Give me hands that remain open to receive. I look forward to moving what fills my hands on to others.

I pray I never fear that time is vanishing—that I will always have time to give and time to spare.

I pray that I'm never too busy to smile, never too busy to share laughter.

I pray that my arms will always hug, my heart will always love. I haven't run out of love yet.

Please allow me to remember that all things are always on "Full" and, if I start fearing emptiness or impoverishment, please help me consider the lilies of the field and remind me that I am a lily.

CHAPTER 21

PEACE AND FREEDOM
ARE PRAYERS

The function of prayer is not to influence God,
but rather to change the nature of the one who prays.

—Søren Kierkegaard, Danish philosopher, theologian

What Is the Meaning of Your Life?

When I was in my twenties, I was deeply influenced by Viktor Frankl's book, *Man's Search for Meaning*. In it he said, "One should not ask 'What is the meaning of life?' But rather, recognize that it is *he* who is asked, 'What is the meaning of *your* life?'" Frankl said, "We must answer by being responsible." We are each responsible for the meaning of our own life. It is life who asks *us*: "What is the meaning of *your* life?"

In the concentration camps in Germany during WWII, Frankl said that what made the difference between those who survived and those who didn't was having something bigger than themselves to live for—something that gave meaning to their lives. For some prisoners, it was their family. They did everything they could to keep on going, despite the horrific conditions and terrible treatment at the hand of their Nazi captors. For others, it was their faith that kept them alive—they believed in God, in a higher power—they believed they needed to carry on the Jewish faith.

For still others, it was their work that gave them reason to live—their art, their writing, or their research that they hoped to continue if they ever got out of the death camps. In short, everyone had something bigger than themselves that gave their life meaning. One had to have a meaning, a purpose in life, in order to keep going. That was their life's work—to serve God, or to serve their family, or to serve the work they were committed to. For these prisoners, survival was their prayer—survival for the sake of a larger cause.

What is it that gives your life meaning? What is your life's work? What is your prayer?

> The purpose of life is not to be happy.
> It is to be useful, to be honorable,
> to be compassionate,
> to have it make some difference that you have lived
> and lived well.

> —Ralph Waldo Emerson

I Find Freedom in Freeing Thoughts

Over the course of my life, I have been driven by wanting to know the "truth." "If I just knew the truth, then I could..." I have learned this idea that the "real truth," the *set-in-concrete unbendable truth*, has some magical qualities of manifestation. I have believed that those eternal truths *must be* the starting line for the *real* journey in life.

Today I find relief in letting go of my search for the truth. My desire is to let go of old historical ideas of the truth and look for thoughts of freedom. I love it when I notice I just declared something to be the real truth and I'm able to recognize it and bless those old thoughts on their way and bless me for thinking them.

If I declare something to be the truth, I shake that off. If I declare, "This is how much money I make," I shake that off. If I believe my businesses can't have a sudden sustained growth spurt, I shake that off. "I don't like to exercise"—I shake that off. I let it go. I may say it again and, when I notice, I shake it off again. In those moments, I have a window of freedom.

In those moments I have a real experience of *now*, of newness, of birth. It starts with the thought that any truth I know, or that so many truths I know, aren't the truth. I find freedom in that. I find excitement in anticipating some new thing that's going to expand my field of experience, though it may very well be that, in time, that would be another "truth" and I will let it go. For the moment, it stretches out the boundaries of my field of experience.

I find freedom in freeing thoughts. What truths am I certain of today? What have I come to believe that "I know beyond a doubt"? What thoughts have I, in some moment of great knowing, set into concrete to make certain they don't float away? When I find such a belief I can, with love for it and for me, imagine that concrete crumbling and that belief vanishing. I can step into that new void and take a deep breath of freedom. Every vanishing belief creates that void and creates that breeze of new freedom, of new life.

I find freedom in freeing thoughts.

I asked for wisdom...

and God gave me problems to solve.

I asked for prosperity...

and God gave me brains and the strength to work.

I asked for courage...

and God gave me danger to overcome.

I asked for love...

and God gave me troubled people to help.

I asked for favors...

and God gave me opportunities.

I received nothing I wanted.

I received everything I needed.

My Prayer has been answered.

—Anonymous (Islamic origin)

What Does Serenity Mean to Me?

Selflessness

Ego-reduction

Real Peace of Mind

Energy for Life

No Drama

Interest in Others

Tranquility

"Yes" to God's Grace and Love

PRAYER

Power Source

God, you are like electricity.
I can't see electricity
    but I know it's real
    because I see its results.
Electricity lights up my home,
    makes my appliances work,
    and powers my computer.
You are like that.
I can't see You but
    I know You're real
    because I see Your results.
You create life,
    make the planets spin in orbit,
    and power my body and mind.
I don't doubt the existence of electricity
    just because it's invisible—
nor do I doubt You
    just because You're invisible.
I wouldn't try to operate my computer
    without plugging it into a power source.
Why would I try to run *my life*
    without tapping into a power source?

—BJ Gallagher

—————————————— PRAYER ——————————————

My Compass Points Toward True Joy

God, my desire is to follow Vision. Today's desire is the map to tomorrow's life. Where am I headed?

I'm not waiting for someone to create the road map to joy. Higher Power, you and I are the map-makers and the trip planners.

Through prayer and meditation I ask you for and receive Vision for what's next. I quiet my mind, I clear the screen. My journey appears before me and I'm ready to go.

This leg of my journey is the best. Always.
The next leg of my journey is the best. Always.
Joy is my destination and
the vehicle that carries me forward.

—————————————— PRAYER ——————————————

Deep, Deep Water

Deep, deep water
And the harbor is wide.
Somewhere storms are raging
But it's peaceful here inside.

My ship is well protected
And sheltered in this port.

My body is well rested and
I'll journey out once more.

And from this Peaceful berth
I'm sailing out again.
I'm seeking new horizons.
I'm bound out with the wind.

I am called into the Great Unknown
By a voice I hear within
And I know this peaceful harbor
Will be here
When I sail back in.
Deep, deep water
And the harbor is wide.

—Sam Beasley

_____ PRAYER _____

Miracles will follow miracles
and wonders will never cease
because all my expectations
are for good.

—Marc Allen, author, poet, songwriter

_____ PRAYER _____

Happiness Is My Prayer

I believe that happiness is my birthright,

as well as my responsibility;

    and I commit to claiming it.

I believe that happiness is here and now;

    and I commit to awakening to it.

I believe that happiness is a choice;

    and I commit to choosing it.

I believe that happiness is a habit;

    and I commit to cultivating it.

I believe that happiness is free,

like rainbows, sunshine, and air;

    and I commit to reveling in it.

I believe that happiness is always available,

no matter what others are doing;

    and I commit to creating it.

I believe that happiness is an inside job,

not dependent on money, fame, or possessions;

    and I commit to living it.

I believe that happiness is an attitude of gratitude;

    and I commit to giving thanks.

I believe that happiness is in action;

    and I commit to generating it.

I believe that happiness is contagious;

and I commit to sharing it.
I believe that happiness is a prayer,
uniting me with the universe;
and I commit to offering it.
I believe that happiness is my calling—
I must be the happiness I wish to see in the world.

—BJ Gallagher

CONCLUSION

My ninety-one-year-old mother has end-stage Alzheimer's. Last December, I was feeding her lunch one day and told her, "Guess what, Mom? Christmas is just two weeks away. Isn't that exciting?"

Without missing a beat, she looked at me and said, "*Every* day is Christmas."

I had to laugh. "Oh you're right, Mom. Silly me, I forgot."

That's my mother's prayer. "Every day is Christmas." That's how she's lived her whole life.

When her caregivers ask, "How do you feel, Gloria?" Mom grins and holds up her hands and says, "I feel with my fingers."

If a visitor says, "Have a good day," Mom always says, "*Every* day is a good day!"

My mother has taught me many things over the years, but the best lesson is "Every day is Christmas!" It's become my favorite prayer. I look for the gifts in every experience. I expect surprises—and sometimes I even get miracles. And I make sure to give presence to my elderly mom—not presents, but *presence*—and presence to everyone else in my life as well. I give them the gift of myself—my time, my attention, my love.

For Mom and me, "Every day is Christmas."

What's your prayer?

AKNOWLEDGMENTS

It takes a village to make a book successful. This book is no exception. We'd like to thank our Mango village: the beautiful and brilliant editor Brenda Knight for shepherding this book into such perfect completion; Morgane Leoni for her simple, elegant, spiritual design; Natasha Vera and Robin Miller for their superb line editing; and Hannah Paulsen, Merritt Smail, and Michelle Lewy for their fantastic, non-stop marketing on behalf of our book.

Special thanks to our publisher and the CEO of Mango, Chris McKenney, who knows what it's like to be a peacock in the land of publishing penguins. In Mango Publishing you have created a true Land of Opportunity—where birds of different feathers can flock and create together. Thank you!

Most importantly, we thank our loved ones—Suzanne Lorenz and Michael Hateley—who inspire our endless prayers of gratitude and joy. We love you!

ABOUT THE AUTHORS

> Spiritual practice is not just sitting and meditating.
> Practice is looking, thinking, touching, drinking,
> eating, and talking.
> Every act, every breath, and every step
> can be practice
> and help us to become more ourselves.
>
> **—Thich Nhat Hanh, Buddhist monk, author,
> teacher**

Sam Beasley

Sam Beasley is a successful businessman entrepreneur who uses spiritual principles to establish and build and run his businesses. He is a charismatic speaker and dynamic workshop leader whose mission is to share what he's learned so that others may become successful and fulfilled as well.

Sam is an experienced counselor who understands how people learn, stretch, and grow—he designs educational programs to maximize the opportunity for everyone to realize their growth potential. Sam works with people from all walks of life, including coaches and therapists, to help them create solvent, successful businesses—encouraging them to in turn support *their* clients in attaining financial and spiritual freedom.

Sam has also been a passionate singer/songwriter for over fifty years and has been blessed to write, perform, and record with many of his musical heroes. He credits his years in the music business with teaching him important lessons about creativity and spirituality.

Sam and his wife, Suzanne Lorenz, have been partners in life and in business for the past thirty years. They have devoted that time to encouraging the public to stop driving under the influence. Sam serves on the Board of Directors of the California Association of DUI Treatment Programs, working to improve the quality of interventions on those who have been arrested for DUIs.

Sam and Suzanne coauthored a book on the connection between financial net worth, psychological and spiritual self-worth, and self-care—*Wealth and Well-Being: How Therapists, Counselors, and Helping Professionals Can Assist Clients through the Emotional Barriers to Financial Independence*—and a companion workbook, *Wealth and Well-Being Workbook: Overcoming Barriers to Financial Independence* (Any Wind Publishing).

Sam's books, like his workshops, are filled with inspirational wisdom, as well as practical how-to tips. Whether his audience is therapists and counselors, creatives who want to make a living with their art, or regular folks who want to enhance their savvy and skill with money, his goal is to help people achieve freedom—freedom from want *and* freedom from fear. Sam teaches and inspires thousands with his wisdom, compassion...and sometimes a song or two as well.

BJ Gallagher

BJ Gallagher is an inspirational speaker and prolific author. She writes business books that educate and empower, women's books that enlighten and entertain, and gift books that inspire and inform. Whether her audience is corporate executives, working women, or job seekers, her message is "The Power of Positive DOING." She motivates and teaches with empathy, understanding, and more than a little humor.

BJ's international business fable, *A Peacock in the Land of Penguins* (Berrett-Koehler) is THE best-selling diversity book in the world—published in twenty-three languages. Her other business books include: *Being Buddha at Work: 108 Ancient Truths on Change, Stress, Money, and Success* (Berrett-Koehler) with a Foreword by the Dalai Lama, *YES Lives in the Land of NO: A Tale of Triumph Over Negativity* (Berrett-Koehler), and a career book, *It's Never Too Late To Be What You Might Have Been* (Viva Editions). Her newest book is *The Leadership Secrets of Oz* (Simple Truths).

BJ's inspirational books include *The Power of Positive Doing* (Simple Truths), *If God Is Your Co-Pilot, Switch Seats* (Hampton Roads), *The Road to Happiness* (Simple Truths), and *Learning to Dance in the Rain* (Simple Truths).

BJ has been featured on *CBS Evening News*, the *Today* show, Fox News, PBS, CNN, and other television and radio programs. She is quoted frequently in various newspapers, women's magazines, and websites, including *O, The Oprah Magazine*, *Redbook*, *Woman's*

World, New York Times, Chicago Tribune, Wall Street Journal, Christian Science Monitor, Orlando Sentinel, Financial Times (UK), *Guardian* (UK), MSNBC.com, CareerBuilder.com, CNN.com, and Forbes.com, among others.

In addition to writing books, BJ also conducts seminars and delivers keynotes at conferences and professional meetings across the country.

Her clients include IBM, Chevron, US Veteran's Administration, John Deere Credit Canada, Volkswagen, Farm Credit Services of America, Raytheon, US Department of Interior, Phoenix Newspapers Inc., the American Press Institute, Infiniti, Nissan, and Atlanta Journal Constitution, among others.